BARRON'S DOG BIBLES

Great Danes

Rachel Cawley and John Cawley

BARRON'S

Acknowledgments

Great Dane owners from around the world throughout the years have generously shared their knowledge about the many varied ways of the Great Dane. Though we cannot list every one of them, we would like to mention Linda Arndt, JP Yousha, Gina M. Jaeblon, Sharon Hladik, and Carolyn Mobley.

About the Authors

Rachel Cawley has been actively involved with the breeding, showing, and training of Great Danes for more than a decade. She enjoys Great Danes as loving family members, as well as being a breeder handling them in conformation and rally. Rachel gained her interest in animals while living on a farm in her youth. She has studied creatures domestic and wild. Rachel has a certification for wildlife rehabilitation and has spent time working alongside veterinarians. She has visited hospitals with therapy animals (including a Great Dane, a cat, and a miniature horse). Rachel is also known as an accomplished artist, creating portraits, pointillism, kennel logos, cartoon art, sculpture, and more. Her work can be found at various Internet locations.

John Cawley has been a writer for more than two decades. He has authored and co-authored numerous books, and his articles have appeared in dozens of publications. John has become a full-time Great Dane dad and enjoys the time he spends with his family—two- and four-legged.

A Word About Pronouns

Many dog lovers feel that the pronoun "it" is not appropriate when referring to a pet that can be such a wonderful part of our lives. For this reason, Great Danes are described as "he" throughout this book unless the topic specifically relates to female dogs. This by no means infers any preference, nor should it be taken as an indication that either sex is particularly problematic.

Cover Credits

Shutterstock: front cover; Tara Darling: back cover

Photo Credits

Kent Akselsen: pages 10, 17, 60, 76, 146, 150; Barbara Augello: pages vi, 148; Seth Casteel: pages 37, 47, 103; Dreamstime: pages 40, 42, 45, 66, 74; Jeanmfolge.com: page 116; iStockphoto: pages i, v, 21, 30, 52, 81, 88, 111, 128; Daniel Johnson/Paulette Johnson: pages 23, 49, 87, 118, 122 (top), 122 (bottom), 123 (top), 123 (bottom), 124 (top), 124 (bottom), 125 (top), 125 (bottom), 126 (top), 126 (bottom), 127 (top), 127 (bottom), 131, 134, 158; Oh My Dog! Photography: pages 39, 80, 84, 115, 145; Shutterstock: pages iii, 2, 5, 13, 14, 19, 22, 25, 26, 29, 32, 35, 48, 55, 56, 57, 68, 69, 71, 73, 83, 92, 95, 96, 99, 105, 106, 137, 138, 141, 147, 152, 155, 160, 162; Kira Stackhouse: pages 63, 65, 78, 100, 121; Connie Summers/Paulette Johnson: page 108; Joan Hustace Walker: pages 112, 132, 133, 143, 156.

All inquiries should be addressed to:
Barron's Educational Series, Inc.
250 Wireless Boulevard
Hauppauge, New York 11788
www.barronseduc.com

ISBN: 978-0-7641-4476-9 (Book)
ISBN: 978-0-7641-8678-3 (DVD)
ISBN: 978-0-7641-9754-3 (Package)

Library of Congress Catalog Card No: 2011026569

Library of Congress Cataloging-in-Publication Data

Cawley, Rachel.
  Great Danes / Rachel Cawley and John Cawley.
    p. cm. — (Barron's dog bibles)
    ISBN 978-0-7641-4476-9 — ISBN 978-0-7641-8678-3
    ISBN 978-0-7641-9754-3 — ISBN 978-1-4380-8020-8
  1. Great Dane. I. Cawley, John, 1954– II. Title.
  SF429.G7C39 2011
  636.73--dc23   2011026569

Printed in China

9 8 7 6 5 4 3 2

CONTENTS

Preface   v

1. All About Great Danes   1

The Birth of the Breed   1
The Name Game   2
The Great Dane Hall of Fame   3
Great Danes on Screens Large and Small   7
Tall Tails   10
A Great Dane Timeline   11
10 Questions People Ask About Great Danes   12

2. The Mind of the Great Dane   15

Who Is a Great Dane?   15
Bigger Is Not Always Better   16
Great Danes and Your Family   20

3. How to Choose a Great Dane   27

Great Dane Colors   27
Searching for a Great Dane   30
What Types of Breeders Are There?   33
Rescue   35
Your First Look at a Puppy   36

4. Caring for a Great Dane Puppy   43

Growing a Great Dane   43
Housetraining   47
Early Health and Nutrition   52
Socialization   62

5. Living with a Great Dane   67

Shopping for Your Great Dane   67
Talking the (Great Dane) Talk   70
Separation Anxiety   75
Behavior Problems and Solutions   77
The Great Dane Senses   78

CONTENTS

6. Health and Nutrition 85

Genetics and a Dane 85
Feeding Your Great Dane 85
Choosing a Veterinarian 91
Doing a Home Checkup 93
Health Concerns 95

7. Training and Activities 101

Training Tools 101
Basic Commands 103
Teaching Tricks 107
Fun for All 109
Danes on Wheels 110
The Good Citizen 114
Sport Competitions 115
Great Danes for Therapy 120

8. Grooming a Great Dane 129

Big-Dog Bathing 129
Hair Care 129
Great Danes and the Dentist 131
Ear Care 132
Pedicures 134
Flea and Parasite Wars 135

9. The Senior Great Dane 139

The Golden Years 139
The Aging Body 140
Caring for the Elder Dane 143

10. The Great Dane Standard 149

Why Is There a "Standard"? 149
Measuring the Great Dane 150
Temperament 155

Resources 157

Index 159

PREFACE

This book is dedicated to all Great Danes: past, present, and future. Often called the "Apollo of dogs" and a "gentle giant," the Great Dane leaves a lasting impression on all who see one. It is not just this giant's size and weight, but their unique mixture of regal appearance, strength, friendly nature, and comic relief that make them unforgettable.

Those meeting a Great Dane for the first time often comment that "this is a real dog." They mention how one does not need to bend over to pet a Great Dane. And should the Great Dane lean against them or sit in their lap, everyone, including the Dane, smiles.

For those hungry to learn more about this "real dog" this book offers a wealth of information with sections on the breed's history, care, feeding, and more. There are tips for locating your own Great Dane, training young and old, and dealing with specific needs. Along with key information, there are more photos and fun facts than a Great Dane could shake a tail at.

This is a book you'll want to fetch again and again.

Chapter One

All About Great Danes

The Great Dane is often referred to as the Apollo of dogs. Apollo, a son of Zeus (king of the gods), was sometimes referred to as the god of the sun or light. He also was linked to truth, prophecy, medicine, and poetry. The breed's majesty and noble stature certainly gives it the statuesque appearance of the Greek gods.

In fact, throughout history, mankind seemed fascinated with dogs of great size and strength. Paintings of giant dogs resembling Great Danes have been found on Egyptian monuments dating as far back as 3000 B.C. Artifacts found around Babylonian temples dated to 2000 B.C. have shown men walking a massive dog that resembles a Great Dane. Chinese literature dated 1121 B.C. mentions canines similar in appearance to Great Danes. A painting dated approximately 1200 B.C. shows Egyptians using Harlequin-colored dogs (white with black patches) that resemble Great Danes. An image similar to a Great Dane even appears on Greek money dated from 36 B.C.

The Birth of the Breed

It should be stated up front that despite its name, the Great Dane did not originate in Denmark. The Great Dane did not immediately appear as the breed seen today. It was created by blending several existing breeds. And even after the breed had begun to be identified, it took some time before people could settle on a name. England and Germany struggled for years to claim the breed for themselves by attempting to name it after their country.

The Great Dane has been recognized as a breed for more than 400 years. The early Great Danes were called Boarhounds for the job they performed: hunting boars. A boar, being strong and swift, demanded a superior dog to hunt it. Records of the time show these early Great Danes to be quite effective.

As the boar population began to fall, the hounds began a new life. By the sixteenth century the English dubbed the breed English Dogges. These large dogs were bred for image and protection. In the late 1600s a German nobleman bred large numbers of the dogs, prizing the biggest and most

1

attractive. These pampered dogs, often adorned with ornate collars, were kept inside homes and called *Kammerhunde*, literally meaning "chamber dogs."

French naturalist Comte de Buffon (1749–1788) gave the breed the name it has today. Buffon authored a massive (more than 35 volumes) natural-history encyclopedia, *Historie Naturalle*. While visiting Denmark, he came across a sleeker version of the Boarhound. Thinking it a Greyhound, the author said the Danish climate caused the Greyhound to become a Grand Danois, a Great Danish Dog. The name has remained despite attempts to rename the breed.

Fun Facts

Hunting Records

In 1563, more than 2,500 boars were hunted down. The number may be less impressive if one considers the ratio of boars to hounds. One hunter, Duke Henry of Braunschweig, showed up at a hunt in 1592 with *600* male Boarhounds!

The Name Game

More than the average breed, the Great Dane has gone through a variety of names. In the 1800s, the dog's name became a point of contention between England and Germany. The first German dog show (1863) featured two similar breeds: the Dannish Doggen and the Ulmer Doggen. By 1876 the judges began to refuse to allow both names, saying that the dogs were the same breed and only the Deutsche Dogge name was to be used. At the 1879 Hanover show it was decided that the lighter-weight dogs would be Ulmer Doggen and the heavier-weight dogs would be Danish Dogs. More confusing was that Brindle Great Danes were called Hatzruden (Wolf Dogs)!

The 1880 publication of Sydenham Edward's encyclopedia *Cynographia Britannica* (an encyclopedia of British dog breeds) lists the "Great Danish Dog" with an illustration. It describes the dog as being a cross between Greyhounds and Mastiffs with usually cropped ears. The text even mentions "a beautiful variety called the Harlequin Dane."

That same year, a meeting of German breeders and judges agreed that the breed developed in Germany was substantially different from the English Mastiffs. The group insisted the name

FYI: A Great Dane by Any Other Name. . .

Here are the names for Great Danes in a few international tongues.

- Great Dane (English-speaking world and Denmark)
- Gran Danés (Spanish- and Portuguese-speaking world, including South America)
- Grand Danois (French-speaking world, Scandinavia in the twentieth century)
- Tanskandoggi (Finland)
- Danubius Dog (Hungary)
- Danua cinsi kopek or Grand Danua (Turkey)
- Danische Dogge or Grosse Danische Yagd Hund (German-speaking world until 1888–1889)

be changed to Deutsch Dogge (German Dog), forbade all other names, and founded the Deutshe Doggen Club of Germany.

A British club for the breed was formed in 1883. The breed was previously shown as German Boarhounds, but it was decided to name the club the Great Dane Club and include all the name variations, including Boarhounds, Tiger Mastiffs, and German Mastiffs. The name change prompted Prince Solins of Prussia to demand that the British club retain the dog's national origin and call it the Great German Dogge Club. The British ignored the request and kept the Great Dane name.

In 1884, English shows began listing the dog as the Great Dane. The club broke with the rest of the world when it ceased cropping the ears in 1894. King Edward VII, then the Prince of Wales, requested that all cropping be stopped. (Since then, many other countries have outlawed the practice of cropping, calling it everything from barbaric to unnecessary surgery.)

The year 1887 found the breed being recognized by the American Kennel Club. In 1889, the Great Dane Club of America (until then the breed was called the German Mastiff) was founded in Chicago. In 1891, the Great Dane Club of Germany accepted an official description or standard for the breed.

The Great Dane Hall of Fame
(some Danes of Fame—in no particular order)

Keystone Teddy Teddy was one of the first stars of Hollywood, appearing in films years before Rin Tin Tin. He was a natural-eared, lightly marked Brindle Great Dane featured in a variety of Mack Sennett's Keystone Films. Appearing in shorts as early as 1917, he earned $35 per week. When Teddy began working in features, he became one of Sennett's highest-paid actors, earning $350 per week. Sometimes referred to as Teddy the Wonder Dog, he retired from films in 1923.

Fridge Cropped Fawn Great Dane "Fridge," aka Best in Show (BIS), Best in Specialty Show (BISS), Best in Futurity (BIF), Champion (CH) Von Shrado's I'm a Knock Out was the number one Great Dane in 1990 and 1992. He also holds the Best of Breed record, with 404 Best of Breed awards. Fridge has been the only Great Dane of the American Kennel Club record to be number one as a veteran (a Great Dane six years of age or older) and in the top 20 for six years. Fridge qualified for the Great Dane Club of America's Hall of Fame twice for siring 30 or more American Kennel Club Champions and for having won 10 Best in Shows. Often breeder-owner handled, Fridge was Great Dane Club of America's Futurity winner in 1987. (Futurity is a show for puppies that are entered by their breeders when the pups are still in the womb. See the Great Dane Club of California website for more information.)

Giant George Giant George (2005–), a natural-eared Blue Great Dane, was awarded two titles from the Guinness Book of World Records in 2010: Tallest Living Dog and Tallest Dog Ever. He measures 43 inches at the shoulder, and weighs 245 pounds. On the way to one of his first official appearances as the record holder, George took up a row of three seats on an airplane.

Scooby-Doo Debuting September 13, 1969, Scooby-Doo is one of the longest-running cartoon characters from the Hanna-Barbera studio. Sort of resembling a Chocolate Merle, Scooby was named by animation legend Joe Barbera based on Frank Sinatra singing "Scooby-dooby-doo" in "Strangers in the Night." Scooby's original design was by Iwao Takamoto, who said he wanted to make Scooby the opposite of the breed standard, so Scooby is not a typical Great Dane in appearance. Since his debut, Scooby has almost never been off the TV screen. He has moved into other media via a series of long-running direct-to-video animated features and several live-action films (where Scooby is done in CGI, computer-generated imagery).

Fun Facts

The First U.S. Great Dane

The Great Dane was not fully recognized in the United States until the formation of the Great Dane Club of America in 1889. Previously they were referred to as German Mastiffs. But there is a record of a Great Dane in the United States back in 1857. That year a dog named Prince, listed as a Great Dane, was shipped from New York to England. How Prince got to America . . . or why he was shipped to England is not known.

Amazing Gracie One of the founding sisters of Three Dog Bakery, Gracie was born November 11, 1989, and was deaf, as well as blind in one eye. Gracie, a natural-eared Merlequin Great Dane, was executive vice president of eating for the bakery. (See the color chart for more details on Merlequins.) Gracie even has a book about her life story. A foundation named after her offers financial assistance to licensed groups that focus on rescuing dogs. Gracie passed away on January 21, 1999.

Just Nuisance Born in 1937, a natural-eared mask-less Fawn Great Dane, Just Nuisance was a therapy dog in every sense of the word. Purchased by Benjamin Chaney, Just Nuisance ended up in Simon's Town, South Africa. There he became known to sailors of the Royal Navy. He followed the sailors around town. He even went onto their ships, where he was frequently in the way—which is how he gained his name. When he was threatened with destruction for riding on Africa's train systems, the sailors got Just Nuisance enlisted in the Royal Navy on August 25, 1939. Just Nuisance received the same benefits as other sailors, including a bed and hat. As part of his life in the Navy, he would stop fights and help drunken sailors find their way back to base. Just Nuisance was buried in April 1944 with full military honors. A statue of him was erected at Jubilee Square in Simon's Town overlooking the bay off the Cape of Good Hope. On April 1, 2000, a Just Nuisance Commemoration Day Parade was held through Simon's Town's main street. The parade has become an annual event.

Damien from the University of Albany In 1965 the University of Albany changed its mascot from Pierre the Pedguin to a Great Dane. (A Pedguin was an imaginary animal from the merged words of *penguin* and *pedogogy* for the team's name, the Pedagogues.) The breed was chosen via a contest in which students submitted ideas. The winning student said she suggested a Great Dane because of their sheer size, weight, strength, courage, speed, character, and stamina. The mascot was nicknamed Damien. In 2004 the school added another Great Dane mascot, a puppy named Lil D. Both Damien and Lil D are erect-eared Fawn Great Danes. A larger-than-life Great Dane bronze statue is on display in the lobby of the university's Recreation and Convocation Center, a gift from the class of 1999.

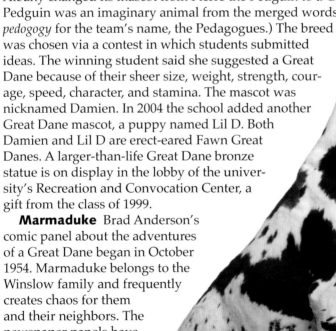

Marmaduke Brad Anderson's comic panel about the adventures of a Great Dane began in October 1954. Marmaduke belongs to the Winslow family and frequently creates chaos for them and their neighbors. The newspaper panels have been reprinted in comic books and paperback collections. In the 1980s, the character starred in a Saturday morning TV series. Anderson acquired a Great Dane bitch in

FYI: Great Danes of the Rich or Famous

- **Otto Von Bismarck**—The famed German politician (credited with unifying Germany in the seventeenth century) had numerous Great Danes. Bismarck's dogs included Sultan, Rebecca, Flora, Freia, and Tyras. A statue of Bismarck and Tyras can be found in Rudelsburg.
- **Jim Carey**—This film star had a black-and-white Great Dane named George, acquired in 2000.
- **Chubby Checker**—Rock-and-roll legend.
- **Fabio**—A famous model and actor, Fabio had Apache, Thor, and Geronimo.
- **June Foray**—The renowned voice actress (Rocky the flying squirrel, Granny in WB cartoons, and more) owned several Great Danes.
- **William S. Hart**—This early film star had several Great Danes in later years. His home, now a national park, has a canine cemetery with tombstones for his pets, including Hamlet and Gall, both Harlequin Great Danes. Hart's home and estate is open for public tours where one can visit his dog's gravestones. There are rumors of workers seeing ghosts of his dogs in the home.
- **Harold Lloyd**—One of the great comics of silent films had Prince.
- **Greg Louganis**—The Olympic Gold Medal diver has bred and owned Harlequin Great Danes.
- **Tom Mix**—One of the earliest cowboy stars, Mix had Duke, who appeared to be a Merle with white markings. He starred with Mix in more than a dozen films.
- **Alexander Pope**—This English poet (1688–1744) owned Bounce, a Great Dane who reportedly saved Pope's life by attacking a knife-wielding assailant. Bounce was also the subject of a poem by poet John Gay, and one of Bounce's pups ended up with the Prince of Wales.
- **Franklin D. Roosevelt**—The U.S. president had a Great Dane named President.
- **Dean Torrance**—Half of rock-and-roll's Jan & Dean, Dean owned Bogie, a Great Dane mix, when he was younger.
- **Andy Warhol**—This iconic artist of the 1960s owned a taxidermied Harlequin Great Dane named Cecil. It was named for (reportedly) former owner, Cecil B. DeMille. Cecil was a model for Warhol, and is on display at the Andy Warhol museum.

the 1990s and named her Marmaladee (pronounced marma-lady). Christine Anderson, his daughter, had a Great Dane of her own named Marmaduchess. In 2010 a feature film was based on the popular character.

Great Dane Trailers Not an official Great Dane, nonetheless, Great Dane Trailers may be the most frequently seen Great Dane in the United States. The well-recognized logo of a stately standing cropped Great Dane is seen on the mud flaps of many trucks on America's highways. In the 1930s, Steel Products Co. hired a respected trailer designer who referred to his trailers as "Great Danes." He was familiar with the breed as work animals known for their strength and stamina. The name stuck, and by 1958, the Steel Production Company changed its name to Great Dane Trailers Inc. At their base in Georgia, a larger-than-life Harlequin statue has stood outside their office for more than 16 years.

MACH Morgan "Danger" Powers This black-and-white natural-eared bitch has more than a dozen titles in areas ranging from agility to flyball. In 2004, she became the first Great Dane to achieve the ultimate agility title, Masters Agility Championship (MACH). Morgan was born in 1999. In 2003, she appeared on two television competitions. Morgan was Miss Colorado for Fox's "Miss Dog Beauty Pageant," and she was part of the winning team in Purina's Incredible Dog Challenge Outdoor Adventure. The latter event had the biggest (Morgan) and smallest dog entered on one team—the Mountain West Altidogs. At 10 years of age, Morgan has headed toward a Rally Novice title. Morgan has also been nominated to the Flyball Hall of Fame. She retired after the 2009 Great Dane Club of California National Specialty Agility Trials. (For more information on Morgan, check out her website at *www.deaspeedwaggin.com/dogs/morgan*.)

Fun Facts

Diamonds Are a Dane's Best Friend?

Evalyn Walsh McLean, an owner of the famed Hope diamond in the early 1900s, reportedly would let her Great Dane, Mike, wear the diamond on walks around town!

Great Danes on Screens Large and Small

Because of their size, Great Danes have been a popular addition to movies, appearing in nearly 100 feature films. Their ability to be goofy or intimidating makes them perfect for laughs or terror. They have shared the big screen with some of Hollywood's biggest stars, such as W.C. Fields, Dean Martin, Jerry Lewis, Bette Davis, Elvis Presley, Bob Hope, Rock Hudson, Jack Lemmon, Spencer Tracy, Jackie Gleason, Mel Gibson, Freddie Prinze Jr., Leslie Nielson, Michael J. Fox, William Shatner, Uma Thurman, and more. Here is a small selection of movie titles you may wish to look for.

- *Teddy at the Throttle* (1917). Keystone Teddy, a lightly marked Brindle Great Dane, is featured in the title of this film that co-stars silent superstar Gloria Swanson. Teddy sings with Gloria, dances with her maid, stops a train, saves the girl from a fortune hunter, and reunites her with the right man in time for the closing credits.
- *Seven Chances* (1925). In this Buster Keaton silent feature, Keaton finds he will inherit a fortune if married by 7 P.M. that day. The leading lady owns a Harlequin Great Dane who steals the ending of the film. Of note, the Great Dane is played by different Harlequins, some cropped and some uncropped!
- *Six of a Kind* (1934). A couple beginning their second honeymoon invites another couple along to save money. The new couple (famed comedians

George Burns and Gracie Allen) bring their Fawn Great Dane, Rang Tang Tang, who insists on sitting in the front seat and causes constant commotion on the trip.

- *Blondie in Society* (1941). This is one of the features based on the popular Blondie comic strip. Dagwood is given a Fawn Great Dane in lieu of money owed. Blondie decides to enter the Dane in a dog show, hoping to win a monetary prize. Meanwhile, it seems everyone wants the Great Dane, who is Champion Chin Up White Tie for Dinner.
- *Hollywood or Bust* (1956). In the duo's final film, Dean Martin and Jerry Lewis drive across the country with Jerry's Fawn Great Dane, Mr. Bascomb. On the way Mr. Bascomb sings with Jerry, drives the car, falls in love with Anita Ekberg's Toy Poodle, and attends a Hollywood premiere. This is a fun film and a great showcase for the breed.
- *The Ugly Dachshund* (1966). This Disney live-action romp has a married couple (Dean Jones and Suzanne Pleshette) raising a Great Dane puppy with a litter of Dachshunds. As the Fawn Great Dane, called Brutus, grows, he creates mischief around the house but wins the day when he wins at a dog show.
- *Live a Little, Love a Little* (1968). Elvis Presley falls for a free-spirited young lady who owns a Fawn Great Dane. In a dream sequence, Elvis sings a song while an actor in a Great Dane costume dances around him.
- *Oliver and Company* (1988). This Disney animated feature tells Dickens's *Oliver Twist* with animals. Oliver is a cat with a gang of pickpocket dogs. One of the canine gang members is Einstein, a Great Dane voiced by Richard Mulligan. Einstein's cartoon color leads one to believe he is closest to being a Blue.
- *Head Over Heels* (2001). An undercover agent walks a neighbor's dog (Fawn Great Dane) that seems overly interested in human females. The Great Dane is sometimes played by a large puppet.
- *Chestnut: Hero of Central Park* (2004). In this family film, orphaned sisters find a Fawn puppy in Central Park. They try to keep him a secret from their new parents, who live in a posh New York apartment that does not allow dogs.
- *Marmaduke* (2010). Based on the popular comic strip, the story has Marmaduke and his family moving from the Midwest to a new home in a trendy Southern California city. There he falls in love, surfs, and takes on a dog-park bully. Marmaduke talks in the film, though he does not in the comic strip.

On the small screen, Great Danes have appeared in several series. Hanna-Barbera's Scooby-Doo is one of the longest-running characters in cartoons, having appeared in a variety of animated series and movies since his debut in 1969. *The Jetsons* starred Astro (whose real name is discovered to be Tralfaz) as the family pet. Diana Rigg had a Great Dane as her pet in the series *Diana*. Great Danes have also been guest stars on such series as *Two and a Half Men, Bewitched, The Man from U.N.C.L.E., I Dream of Jeannie, ALF, Judging Amy, Walker, Texas Ranger,* and *The Honeymooners*.

FYI: The Dane in Print

The Great Dane's size and royal appearance have made him popular with authors and cartoonists. Here are several books that feature the breed:

- *The Ugly Dachshund* (1938). Written by Gladys Bronwyn Stern and first published in 1938, the book tells of a Great Dane raised with a family of Dachshunds. In the book, the animals talk to each other (unlike the Disney film of 1966). The Dane wonders why he is treated differently from the other Dachshunds in the house . . . and why "the great dog" in the mirror comes to look at him.
- *The Great Dane Thor* (1966). Written by Walter Farley, of Black Stallion fame, the story follows the struggles of a young boy and his father's Great Dane. The dog has killed wildlife around the farm, and the boy fears it. However, the father insists that the boy rehabilitate the dog.
- *The Invisible Dog* (1995). Written by Dick King-Smith, the story follows a young girl who creates an imaginary, invisible dog, Henry. Henry is a Harlequin Great Dane . . . that seems to be coming to life.
- *Harry Potter and the Sorcerer's Stone* (1997). Fang, Hagrid's dog, is described in the book as a "Boarhound," or Great Dane. It is only in the movies that he is portrayed as a Neapolitan Mastiff.
- The Pinkerton Series. In 2002 Steven Kellogg debuted his first illustrated story about Pinkerton, the Harlequin Great Dane—*Pinkerton, Behave!* The series includes such titles as *Prehistoric Pinkerton*, *A Penguin Pup*, and *A Rose for Pinkerton*. Pinkerton is based on an actual Harlequin Great Dane that Kellogg owned.
- *The Guardian* (2004). Written by Nicholas Sparks, this is a suspenseful tale of a widow with a gift of a Great Dane from her late husband. When a suitor shows interest in the widow, the Great Dane senses danger and does his best to protect her.
- *Return to Howliday Inn* (2007). Part of the popular Bunnicula series by James Howe, this recent installment has the cat-and-dog detecting duo of Chester and Harold meet up with a Great Dane named Hamlet while solving another mystery.

They even pop up in music videos. Lady Gaga has featured Harlequin Great Danes in several of her music videos. Two of the Great Danes frequently used have been Lava (CH. PCH It's What's Shakin) and her son Rumpus (CH PCH Start the Commotion). A Harlequin Great Dane is also seen in Soundgarden's "Black Hole Sun" music video.

Great Danes have also proved to be great TV commercial icons. In 2007 a Harlequin Great Dane became official spokes-dog for Pergo (a flooring company), appearing in print and on TV. The dog was portrayed by Shine (registered name: CAN/UKC/INT Champion Morning Star's Walkin' on Sunshine), a Harlequin that had been painted to match the corporate logo. A few other nonpet-product companies using Great Danes have been Thomasville Furniture, Saturn, Hallmark, and Taco Bell.

Tall Tails

The Guinness Book of World Records is no stranger to Great Danes, as to date four have held big titles with them. Each one, interestingly enough, hails from the United States of America.

In 2004 an uncropped Harlequin Great Dane from California by the name of Gibson was recognized by the Guinness Book of World Records as the world's Tallest Living Dog. Gibson was 42.2 inches tall at the top of his shoulder and weighed 170 pounds. In 2009 Gibson had a leg amputated because of bone cancer and, sadly, succumbed to the disease a few months later.

In 2009 another dog residing in California was awarded the Guinness Book of World Records title of world's Tallest Living Dog. This was Titan, an uncropped White Great Dane who measured 42.25 inches at the top of his shoulder. This 190-pound rescued Great Dane was blind, deaf, and epileptic.

In 2010 an Arizona dog named Giant George became the title holder of the Guinness Book of World Records' Tallest Living Dog. George did more than that, though; he was also certified as the Guinness Book of World Records Tallest Dog Ever. Giant George is an uncropped Blue Great Dane who weighs 245 pounds and stands 43 inches tall at the top of his shoulder.

In 2011 the Guinness Book of World Records added a new title, separating the world's Tallest Living Dog category by sex. An Illinois-residing uncropped Mantle Great Dane bitch by the name of Nova was the first bestowed the title of world's Tallest Living Female Dog. Nova measured in at 35.51 inches from the floor to the top of her shoulder and weighs 160 pounds.

A Great Dane Timeline

1749—French Naturalist Comte de Buffon begins publishing his *Historie Naturalle*. In the book he describes seeing a large, sleek Boarhound while visiting Denmark. He refers to it as "a Great Danish dog."

1857—A printed record shows that a "Great Dane" dog is shipped from the United States to England.

1880—Breeders and judges in Berlin agree that a new breed is substantially different from the English Mastiffs and names it Deutsch Dogge (German Dog).

1887—The breed is recognized by the American Kennel Club, though it is initially called the German Mastiff.

1889—The Great Dane Club of America is formed, and becomes only the fourth breed club to become affiliated with the American Kennel Club (which had, itself, formed only five years previously).

1917—A lightly marked Brindle Great Dane called Keystone Teddy is a silent film star, possibly the first canine superstar.

1937—Just Nuisance, a Fawn Great Dane, is born and later becomes the first dog to be enlisted in the Royal Navy.

1954—Marmaduke, the Great Dane star of his own comic strip, debuts in newspapers across the country.

1965—The Great Dane is designated the official state dog of Pennsylvania.

1969—Scooby-Doo, an animated Great Dane, debuts on TV.

1980—CH Sterling's Blue Lupine becomes the first uncropped (natural-eared) Blue AKC Champion Great Dane.

1999—The color Mantle is officially accepted by the AKC. That same year, CH Harlwood Dark Horse becomes the first Mantle AKC Champion Great Dane.

2004—Gibson, a Harlequin Great Dane, is recognized by the Guinness Book of World Records as the world's "tallest living dog" at 42.2 inches. This begins a string of Great Danes holding the title. (For more See Chapter 10 "The Great Dane Standard.")

2006—Multi-titled Sterling Lazy Days Chntly Lace becomes the first Great Dane to earn the title of AKC Obedience Trial Champion.

10 **Questions** People Ask About Great Danes

1 **What are the "colors" of the Great Dane?** The colors found in Great Danes are basically formed from black, tan, and white. These three basics can be combined to just about any variation. However, there are six standard color styles taken from show conformation guidelines. They are Black, Blue (actually gray), Fawn (golden brown), Brindle (black and brown), Harlequin (white with black patches and occasional merle patches), and Mantle (black with specific white areas). They can also come in just about every other mixture—but such colors would not be conformation show dogs.

2 **How much does a Great Dane weigh?** A full-grown Great Dane male typically weighs between 130 and 175 pounds. A full-grown Great Dane bitch typically weighs 100–140 pounds. (Males usually are taller and heavier than females.) Based on the dog's bone structure and build, it could weigh more or less.

3 **Is the Great Dane from Denmark?** The Great Dane is mostly a mix of English and German breeding. The name comes from a famed naturalist of the 1700s. While on a trip to Denmark, he saw the large breed and described it as a "great Danish dog." Despite attempts from Germany and England to attach their own names, the "Great Dane" comment stuck, and by 1900 it was the established name.

4 **Why were the ears cropped?** Since Great Danes were bred as boarhounds, their ears were cut very short and close to their skulls to prevent them from becoming handles that boars could latch onto and tear. Today it is basically a cosmetic effect.

5 **Is that a Dalmatian?** Although most people are familiar with what a fawn Great Dane looks like, a Harlequin often puzzles them. Harlequins may be white with black markings like a Dalmatian, but that coloring is the only similarity. Unlike a Dalmatian, which has spots, a Harlequin has irregularly shaped patches with jagged, torn-looking edges. Plus, an adult Great Dane is much taller and heavier.

6 **How big is a Great Dane when born?** Despite their giant adult size, Great Dane puppies often weigh between 1 and 2 pounds at birth.

7 **Do Great Danes need a lot of space?** Great Danes may love to run, but they often love to lie around. Because of his easygoing style, and couch pup-tato desires, many consider Great Danes to be one of the best dogs for apartments.

8 **Can my child ride a Great Dane?** Though he may be as big as a pony, he is not one. His structure is not built to carry weight. However, Great Danes can be trained to pull a cart, and actually did pull milk carts in some European countries.

9 **Are Great Danes the tallest breed of dogs?** Even though the last few Guinness Book of World Record holders for tallest dog have been Great Danes, the Great Dane is not normally the tallest dog. The AKC standard for a male Great Dane is no less than 30 inches (with 32 inches or more being preferred), with the average-sized male around 34–36 inches tall. Bitches are generally shorter. Great Danes, and dogs in general, are like people—size can vary greatly.

10 **How long do Great Danes live?** On average, Great Danes live around eight years. Some have lived into double digits, but one should not expect it. However, their short life span is in reverse proportion to the huge amount of love they give.

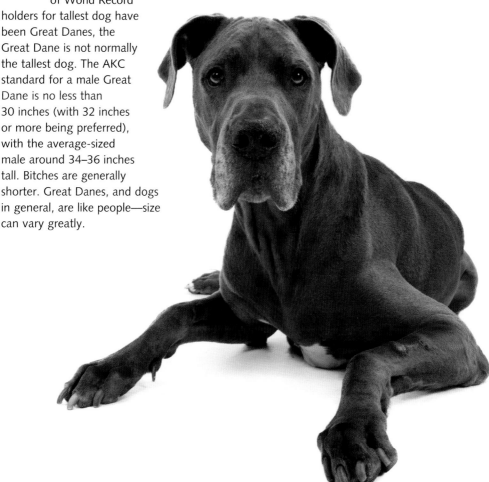

Chapter Two

The Mind of the Great Dane

T he size of a Great Dane is equal to the size of his heart, and of the love and companionship he can offer. Whether bounding along a beach, trotting by your side in a show, enjoying a toy, or curled up next to you on a couch or bed, there is nothing like a Great Dane.

Who Is a Great Dane?

Great Dane personalities can vary as widely as humans'. They can be a clown, a lover, an adventurer, a thinker, a show-off, a brat, or a blend of all the above. But beneath all these variations is still the original Great Dane, bred for hunting and protection. In some ways, you can divide the Great Dane world into two views—those who still hold to the ways of the hunt and show a noticeable prey drive, and those who have moved on and are happy being loved pets.

The Great Dane will find his size a blessing and a curse. He will enjoy the advantages of his size when wanting to obtain things out of reach of smaller creatures (even children). One need not have to bend over to pet or feed a Great Dane. And, unless trained otherwise, he will easily snatch items from table and countertops. (Be aware that some of these items may be harmful to him.) Along with the size of their bodies comes the equally large size of your bills for feed, toys, and health care.

Yet this large size may confuse him. Suddenly, things that were easy as a puppy, such as fitting in a bed, or walking in narrow spaces, or picking up small toys, seem to be more of a challenge as he grows. In some ways, while the size of a Great Dane increases, his perception of the world does not always follow. At 100-plus pounds, he will still think nothing of wanting to sit in your lap, curl up in your favorite chair, or leap about in the house.

Another aspect of his ancestral personality is the desire to serve. Whether taking commands in the hunt or residing next to royalty, the Great Dane has a natural desire to follow commands. This can make the Great Dane an easily trainable breed. Yet his easygoing, big-oaf, couch-potato personality may challenge the teacher.

BE PREPARED! Great Dane = Great Expenses

Owning a giant breed can be harder on the pocketbook than a smaller breed. Be certain that you are prepared for all the costs associated with pet ownership.

- Purebred Great Dane puppies can begin at $500 and can easily go into the thousands, depending on bloodlines, color, show potential, and so on.
- Getting a pre-owned Great Dane or Great Dane mix can cost around $100 to $400. Helping a dog getting a new start can be great. One caveat to remember is that a dog that has had previous owners may have unknown issues, from personality to health.
- Adult Great Danes eat a lot. Puppies require a good deal of food as growth demands. Expect to spend around $30 per month for poor-quality food, $50 per month for good-quality food, and $80 per month for high-quality food.
- The first years will be one of the most expensive. Puppy growth requires possible vaccines and neutering/spaying. There may also be obedience classes. All of this can total $1,000 or more.
- An average adult year can include basic veterinarian bills (vaccine boosters, pest control, and so on), boarding, licensing (varies by location), and so on. Depending on your area and medical routine the annual costs can range from $300 to $500.
- Ideally your Great Dane will live to a ripe old age with few problems. But the truth is that as age approaches, everyone's costs (people's and pets') can rise. Procedures, medications, and care can easily add up to an additional $500 or even much more.
- Of course there is always the unexpected. Accidents, illness, and emergency surgeries can all prove to be quite expensive. For example, cost for a gastric volvulus and dilatation after bloat can run $3,000 to $5,000.

Someone planning on purchasing a Great Dane should plan on at least $15,000 over the pet's lifetime.

Despite his heritage as a hunter, the modern Great Dane is more of a companion that prefers to simply "hang" with his owner. He will fret when you are not home. He may try to sit with you on the couch or lie with you in bed. It is simply his way of showing his devotion to you.

Bigger Is Not Always Better

Great Danes can make wonderful companions. They are affectionate and desire to be with you. As many will tell you, Great Danes are "a real dog." Great Danes touch your heart. Those who own one often want another. Those who have had a Great Dane in the past will talk lovingly of their lost friend even though it may have been decades ago. However, despite all of the charm and pleasures a Great Dane can offer, the breed is not necessarily perfect for everyone.

PERSONALITY POINTERS
Great Dane Body Language

Mood	Friendly	Curious or Excited	Playful
How he holds his head	Normal posture and head position	Extended neck and possible tilted head	"Play bow," chest and head down, rump in air
His eyes	Wide open	Wide open or possibly squinting	Wide open
His ears	Alert, forward, or off to the side	Perked forward	Alert, forward, or off to the side
His mouth	Mouth open, tongue often in a "smile"	Mouth partially open, one side of lip may be raised	Mouth open, tongue often in a "smile"
His body	Relaxed posture or wiggling with excitement, hopping	Relaxed posture	Chest lowered to ground, rump elevated
His tail	Wagging	Wagging, may pause between wags	Whipping from side to side

A Great Dane is a giant breed. He is not the type you can pick up and carry around when needed, even as a puppy. His weight gives him considerable force when walking, running, or sitting. His size can make it difficult to easily navigate narrow spaces. The adult Great Dane can reach just about any tabletop or counter. His wagging tail can knock a 5-pound object off a table. And though he can be graceful, he can also be a klutz, bumping into walls and furniture, while stepping (or "stomping") on items on the ground or floor—including your feet.

You will find Great Danes to be very social. They will not do well with constant isolation for long hours. Although you cannot be expected to give up your job and social life for a Great Dane, you must remember that this breed is a companion animal and will need some form of company, even if it is simply another pet.

Apprehensive or Anxious	Fearful	Subordinate
Neck stiff, head may be pulled back slightly or lowered to shoulder	Neck stiff, head may be pulled back slightly or lowered to shoulder	Head slightly lowered to shoulder height
Wide open, eyes may wander	Eyes wide, whites of eyes may show, may try to look away	Eyes partially closed
Pulled back	Ears pulled back or flattened against skull	Ears flattened against skull
Mouth slightly open with random tongue licking	Mouth slightly open with random tongue licking	Lips of mouth pulled back in "grin," may lick or nuzzle
Arched back, may be bristled	Arched back, may be bristled from shoulder to tail	May crouch, crawl, expose underbelly, or urinate
Partially lowered, possibly tucked	Tucked tightly to belly	Lowered between legs

Great Dane Issues

When you plan to add a Great Dane to your life, be fully aware of the giant responsibility you are taking on and things you need to consider:

- Great Danes have a relatively short life span—usually 7–10 years.
- You need a stable housing situation. If you move frequently, it may not be easy to find a rental place that will accept any dog, let alone one so large.
- You need enough time. Great Danes are social animals and will be very unhappy, and possibly destructive, if forced to live by themselves or be left alone for long periods of time.
- He needs proper training. Any giant breed must behave, and as he grows into his full giant breed size, proper training will be essential to maintaining a happy home.
- Transportation. Your vehicle must accommodate a Great Dane's size for necessities such as veterinarian visits and general outings.

Some Great Danes can be quite prolific in the drool department. These dogs can fling frothy saliva all over the place, giving their personal decorative flair of drool-sicles. One might be surprised at the range and even height that a Great Dane's flingers can fly. These slimy tossings can even land in your hair—not to mention the fact that after drinking, he can be a veritable waterfall.

Not only that, but a Great Dane's tail is a potential weapon that can make your home look like a murder scene. When he wags his tail and it hits solid objects (walls, tabletops, and doors) or edged objects (such as furniture corners and fences), his tail's end can split (or break open) and begin bleeding. Each wag afterward sprays red beads of blood over walls, furniture, clothing, and you.

This breed can easily knock over or injure those who are either not steady enough or quick enough, such as children or the elderly. His size, his wagging tail, his jumping up, his excitement at company, and such can make him a hazard in your home as he knocks down folks with less-than-perfect balance. Of course, you could always relegate him to a crate or another room, but then you risk the chance of him vocalizing so much that hearing conversations may be difficult. This is why basic training is essential. (See Chapter 7.)

Great Danes and Your Family

Adding a pet to the family is just like adding another family member. And a Great Dane puppy can be as much work as a young child, sometimes more. A growing puppy will demand time, time that may have been previously spent with other family members. This can, in some cases, cause jealousy or resentment. Be certain that everyone in the family is part of the puppy-raising process and understands that the new family member has needs that must be met too.

Your Children . . .

Great Danes generally enjoy children. Young family members frequently have more time to spend with him, and thus give him time to play, cuddle, and even get snacks (like the food kids don't want to eat). There is also a kindred spirit between the young and canines. Perhaps it is because dogs are, as mentioned elsewhere, forever young wolves. Despite their love of children, and vice versa, Great Danes may not always be the best mix in a house of young children.

Young children can easily be knocked down by a Great Dane simply bumping the child. Their small hands and feet are ready targets for a growing dog's less-than-accurate footing. A wagging puppy tail can strike the unintended and easily bruise or knock down toddlers. And a happy tail slap to the eyes, face, or other tender spots can cause pain and possible serious injury.

Playing may attract his attention, causing him to become a locomotive barreling in their direction. When you are playing with your children, he will want similar attention and try to get it via pushing, licking, barking, and other behaviors that may hurt or startle youngsters.

Your Pets . . .

Great Danes are social beings that enjoy company, and that company can include other family pets. There are numerous stories about Great Danes happily living with pets of all sizes, including smaller dogs, cats, horses both big and miniature, rabbits, wallabies, and more. If you already have pets in your house, you will need to be certain to introduce your new family member in a safe, secure fashion.

How a specific dog reacts to other animals will depend a lot on how he was brought up. If he was exposed to creatures of varying size and species, he should not find other pets unusual. He may even see them as members of the pack or as friends. However, if he has experienced only humans, then he may be suspicious, worried, or frightened, or feel threatened by other animals. He may see smaller creatures as toys, which could lead to a bad situation. As with any creature, the earlier in his life you can arrange such an introduction, the better.

Just because a Great Dane is a dog does not mean he will automatically be accepted by other dogs. Being a hound by nature, and a pack animal at heart, Great Danes are mostly gentle souls. They are generally nonaggressive, but because of their immense size other dogs may be intimidated by them. A smaller dog may try showing its dominance by barking or acting aggressive. Your Great Dane may respond with a bark or stare. This can create situations in which the larger dog may be seen as the big bad bully picking on a little dog.

If you are introducing a Great Dane to a canine already in your family, let them meet in a neutral area. Any place in your home is not neutral ground; outside the home or yard is. You may wish to have both on leashes to have more control of the situation. A rambunctious puppy can upset an older dog that may not be up to its monkeyshines. In general, though, many adult dogs will accept that a puppy is a baby and therefore may allow it to do puppy things—up to a point.

When dealing with a new puppy and current canine family member, remember that the elder should receive proper respect. Greet the elder first. Feed the elder first. Do not allow the puppy free access to the older dog's toys or bed area. And should the Great Dane puppy disobey proper canine protocol, causing the older dog to growl or correct the puppy, do not scold the older dog, as he himself is aiding in training. It is important that all canine members of a home create

Breed Needs

Great Danes Are Family, Not Fads

Adding a dog to the household is like adding a new family member. His arrival will change the routine requirements of those in and even outside the home. For this very reason, much thought and planning must be given before getting a Great Dane, or any dog. Great Danes should never be gotten on a whim, given as a surprise gift, or used as a lesson.

COMPATIBILITY Is a Great Dane the Best Breed for You?

SPACE REQUIREMENTS ● ●
Though big in size, Great Danes do not require a lot of space. In fact, because of their often quiet demeanor, they are frequently rated as one of the best breeds for apartments.

EXERCISE REQUIREMENTS ● ●
You might hear folks ask if you have "a lot of space" for your Great Dane to run. Although he may want to stretch his legs on occasion, many Great Danes do not require continuous exercise.

TRAINING ● ● ●
Though often seen in cartoons and films as slow learners, Great Danes can be taught. But because of their size, one must train them early and thoroughly. A full-grown Great Dane that misbehaves can be more than just a nuisance; he can be a hazard.

GROOMING ●
Great Danes are pretty much "wash and wear" because of their short coats. The only factor is that their size means there is more to care for.

SHEDDING ● ●
Although a Great Dane has short hair, they do shed twice a year. Generally, the white hairs are the ones that are the most visible on clothing, furniture, and such.

ENERGY LEVEL ● ● ●
Depending on the breeding and temperament, some Great Danes are quite calm and need little activity, whereas others seem constantly in motion. Watch the parents for some indication of the direction your puppy will take.

AFFECTION LEVEL ● ● ● ●
Great Danes are certainly "people" dogs, as most love the companionship of humans. But because of breeding and raising techniques, you can find some more aloof. At the puppy stage, look for ones that come to you for attention.

4 Dots = Highest rating on scale

a proper pack order to maintain a stable relationship. However, it is also important that the older dog never be allowed to bully the puppy. The key word is *balance*.

Got cats? Unlike the cliché, dogs and cats really can get along. In fact, the casual, relaxed nature of some Great Danes can fit right into the world of felines. However, such friendships are not automatic. When your Great Dane and cat first meet, make sure that the cat has every opportunity to get away. During this introduction you may consider having your Great Dane on a leash, in a crate or secured ex-pen, or in a gated off-room while your cat is free to come and go at will. Some cats may be inquisitive and choose to check out the new family member. Other felines may be less happy and lash out, clawing your Great Dane's face. Such a meeting should be supervised to help keep the peace and prevent injury. If things are going well, you may wish to reward good behavior with small quick-to-eat treats along with praise. Keeping such treats tiny can help prevent one animal from stealing the other's.

If you have smaller pets like rats, guinea pigs, and such, remember that a Great Dane has a big size advantage over them. To avoid "accidents" it is best to be sure the smaller ones have easy-to-reach places to get away from giant feet and bodies. A Great Dane plopping his 100-plus-pound body down on the floor would be bad for any small animal that cannot get out of the way. As always, try to introduce your smaller furred family members to the dog sooner rather than later. This will begin to build awareness between them. Also, the sooner he realizes that these are members of the family, and not strangers, toys, or pests, the better.

Are feathered friends a part of your family? Small birds (finches, canaries, and so on) may be too frail to live in the same room as a Great Dane. His bark and sudden movements may be too startling for them. Large birds, such as parrots, can bite very hard and cause him to retaliate or become frightened of the bird. Just as every Great Dane has a slightly different personality, so will the bird. Generally, it may be safer to keep your birds caged when your Great Dane is in the room.

In most cases, your new Great Dane will become good friends with all the members of the family, two legged or four. Of course, like people, it may take some time for everyone to warm up to each other. But if proper introductions are accomplished, and proper ranking is established, you should have one great happy family.

Chapter Three

How to Choose a Great Dane

Because of the size of the breed, many people may have never seen a Great Dane in person. As a rule, larger breeds are not as common in cities and suburbs as smaller ones. When trying to find your Great Dane, it may take a bit of work. You may not find them immediately in your local newspaper (a once common place to locate a pet or show dog). It is more likely you will locate one through the Internet, local groups, or perhaps magazines.

The key to remember is that "finding" a Great Dane is very different from "choosing" one. It is very easy to fall in love with every puppy you see. With some preparation, research, and consideration, you can increase the chances of finding a family member that will fit your life perfectly for years to come.

Great Dane Colors

Although the American Kennel Club recognizes only six conformation show colors, Great Danes can come in a wide selection of pet color variations.

The Basic Great Dane Colors

There are currently six colors/patterns that are accepted for conformation showing at AKC-sanctioned events. If you are looking to show your Great Dane in conformation shows (judging the dog on appearance, structure, and movement), you need to look within these six color groups.

- **Black**—A Black Great Dane is one with a deep, jet-black-colored coat.
- **Blue**—A Blue Great Dane is one with a dark steel gray, almost metallic color of coat.

Breed Truths

The six conformation show colors of Great Danes accepted by the American Kennel Club are (in alphabetical order)

- Black
- Blue
- Brindle
- Fawn
- Harlequin
- Mantle

- **Brindle**—Somewhat tiger-like in their appearance, a Brindle Great Dane typically has a yellow gold base coat with dark black striping in a chevron pattern and a black face called a mask. A Brindle may vary in its colorization. Often referred to as a "Reverse" or "Onyx" Brindle, it has a dark base coat with lighter golden striping and a black mask.
- **Fawn**—A Fawn Great Dane is the color most commonly recognized in the breed. It is typically a golden base coat with a black face called a mask.
- **Harlequin**—This is a dog of Black, Merle, and White together. A Harlequin Great Dane has a white base coat and black torn-looking patches irregularly placed upon its body. Some merle (light to dark gray, often resembling an oil stain) patches are expected.
- **Mantle**—A Mantle Great Dane is one whose pattern resembles that of a Boston Terrier. (This color was originally referred to as a Boston.) This color of Great Dane is black and white, typically having a black skull and body, whereas his muzzle, throat, collar region, chest, feet, legs, and tail tip are white. Unlike Harlequins, the Mantle must be only black and white, with no merle on them whatsoever. (A merle patch would classify the dog as a heavily marked or "blanketed" Harlequin, not a true Mantle.) One may wonder why this color is called a Mantle. It could be that they are named after a Mantle, which is a piece of clothing similar to a robe, left open in the front and often sleeveless. Hence the black of the dog is the robe.

Helpful Hints

Love at First Sight

When looking at a puppy, remember to ask, "Why do I want a Great Dane?"

- For shows? Then be sure to select for color, conformation, and an outgoing personality.
- For a family pet? Then look for one that is friendly and attentive.
- For a companion for other pets? Then look for one that is friendly and social, not dominant.

Getting a pet should never be an impulse decision. Take some time to think and talk with family and friends. And above all, remember that sometimes, despite all planning, the dog chooses you.

Color Variations

Just because a Great Dane isn't one of the six show colors does not mean he isn't a Great Dane. Neither does this mean that he is "rare" or "exotic"; he is simply considered a pet color.

Pet colors can and often do come from even the best of show-color breedings.

Below are just a few companion color varieties that Great Danes can come in.

- **Merle**—Merle is one of the most common nonshow colors. This dog is typically, but not always, a shade of gray base coat with black patches. Frequently, Merles have white markings on their chest and toes. If a Merle has large amounts of white so that it resembles a Mantle, it is referred to as a Mantle Merle. Merles commonly come from Harlequin breedings.
- **Merlequin**—This describes a white base coat with primarily Merle (gray with black speckling) patches.
- **Mismarked Black**—Sometimes referred to as a Tuxedo Black, it resembles a Black Great Dane wearing a suit. This is often what people call a Black that has too much white on it to be considered a Black yet not enough in specific areas to be classified as a Mantle. White markings are typically on the throat, chest, and paws.
- **Piebald**—Often considered the extreme white version of Mantle, this Great Dane color has a white base coat, a black skull, and a few roundish black patches on its body. Frequently, one of these round patches is at the base of the tail. Some Piebalds, or "pieds" as they are sometimes called, have small round spots on their skin visible through the coat, resembling an English pointer.
- **Fawnequin**—Like the name may suggest, this color resembles a Harlequin with a white base color. However, it has fawn and black coloration in it.
- **White**—Typically, this describes a Great Dane that lacks a good deal of pigment, such as less than 15 percent of the pigment found in average dogs. Great Danes like these may be prone to health-related problems such as blindness or deafness. These dogs are *not* albinos. Albinos lack pigment and therefore have red eyes. Whites' eyes are often blue.

Searching for a Great Dane

Once you have concluded that a Great Dane is for you, where to get your Great Dane puppy is the most important decision you can make. Along with factors such as cost and availability, you need to consider health and temperament. You will not have to look far for advice on how to choose a puppy. There are multiple books, websites, businesses, and more that will be glad to offer their opinion on how to choose.

The first step to searching for a Great Dane is to ask yourself what kind of Great Dane will fit your family. Are you looking for a pet? Do you want to get involved with showing your Great Dane in conformation? Does the idea of competing in canine agility sports interest you? Once answered, these will help you ask the right questions of breeders or other sources for your Great Dane.

Surfing for Danes

Today, the Internet is the number one source for all things, even puppies. One can locate breeders, breed clubs, sites that point you to breeders, and more. This explosion of options can actually increase the difficulty of finding a Great Dane.

The accessibility of the Internet allows for all breeders and sellers to reach a much wider base. It is now possible to purchase puppies from other states and even other countries. (Getting a puppy from a great distance is not always easy, though, so be sure to know where the breeder actually is.) Sadly, it is not always easy to distinguish caring, high-quality breeders from those

that are puppy mills. Many sites offering "pet finding" services do not fully research the quality of the sites they link to.

So just finding a breeder is not enough. You may need to do some further research into your potential source. Try to find out how many years the breeder has been in Great Dane breeding. More than ever, you will want to check into the pedigree of the puppy. You should also look into how many litters they produce each year. If they are breeding more than three litters a year, that could be a warning sign. That said, some high-quality breeders co-own several of their pups every year. They mentor and co-breed these puppies with their owners, which can result in many litters a year. That is why it is wise to research fully before passing judgment.

The Great Dane Club of America's website offers a list of Great Dane breeders who are members. This is a great resource and starting point if seeking a show dog. There is general information, including contact information, on each breeder. However, the site does say that the information has not been verified. You can also search for a state club, which may also have a list of breeders. (For example, the Great Dane Club of California has such a list.)

Breed Truths

One-of-a-Kind Color

Great Danes are the only dog breed that comes in the Harlequin color pattern. At one time, Miniature Pinschers also appeared in this variation, but the color in that breed was bred out and is now quite uncommon. Why is this color pattern referred to as Harlequin? It could be that it is named after Arlecchino (Harlequin in English), a servant so poor that his clothes were old and patched together to the point that they lost their original color. Arlecchino could not read or write so made his meager living as an acrobat and a clown. Hence the term *Harlequin* came to represent entertainers dressed in patches. Some people say Harlequin Great Danes take after Arlecchino with their clownish antics.

Other Search Options

Local Great Dane clubs can also be a good resource. You can find local clubs at *www.gdca.org/gdclubs.htm*. These clubs often have events and shows at which you have the opportunity to meet Great Dane owners, breeders, and their dogs in person. If you cannot find a local Great Dane club, look for an all-breed club. You can find various local clubs and events at the American Kennel Club website (*akc.org*). Even if it is not a Great Dane club, many dog people have friends with other breeds and may be able to assist you.

Other possibilities for locating breeders include websites and magazines. *The Great Dane Gazette* is available in both print and online—check it out at *www.greatdanegazette.com*. The American Kennel Club offers *The AKC Gazette* and a website (*akc.org*) that offers lots of information on dogs. Two online Great Dane magazines are *The Great Dane Review* (*www.greatdanereview.com*)

Fun Facts

Toon Dane
Color Confusion

Scooby-Doo may be the most famous of all Great Danes, but you won't find a real one colored like him. Scooby's base color could be considered a Chocolate, but his back carries a few black patches. Although Chocolate is a possible pet color of Great Danes, genetically they lack black pigment, so they cannot have black markings.

and *Dane World Online* (*www.daneworld.com*). Internet search engines will locate Great Dane groups or forums such as Danes Online (*danesonline.com*) and Leans N Slobbers (*www.leansnslobbers.com*). Also look for e-mail lists to join through groups on Yahoo, Facebook, and other social sites.

Newspapers, once the place where everyone used to advertise litters, are not always the best source. Many of the people who place local ads are backyard breeders. These are typically families with one or two Great Danes they in turn bought from a newspaper classified. They often say the dogs are "registered" or "purebred." Be aware that such ads may be from folks who do not understand the importance of temperament and health—or may not care. Ask to see the parents. Check the pedigree and the puppy's medical records. Though it is not impossible to find a good companion in the newspaper, more frequently they are stories of heartbreak waiting to happen when health issues rise and medical bills become enormous.

What Types of Breeders Are There?

Breeders are people. They breed dogs for many reasons. Some do it to improve the breed lines. Some do it for sport to build a line of champions. Some do it for fun, because they love puppies around the house. Some do it merely for profit.

Professional Breeders Professional breeders are those who have made the showing and breeding of Great Danes their life. Many have been doing it for decades, even generations. These folks pride themselves in breeding only the finest show dogs. You often find them advertising in breed-specific publications or websites. Most have websites focusing on awards their dogs have won. If your goal is a Great Dane for the show ring, you may wish to look into one of these high-profile kennels. Just be aware that such breeders will command top prices. They may also have strict requirements, including demands to show the dog, specific diets, medical requirements, and co-ownership requests.

Hobby Breeders Hobby breeders are a great source between the professional and the backyard breeder. As hobbyists, they often have a natural interest in the history and care of their puppies. Many hobby breeders produce puppies first for themselves. They frequently will have websites full of photos of their dogs and puppies. The sites will emphasize quality as well as awards their dogs may have won. Some will have additional information on the breed. Hobby breeders are often more accessible and open to first-time buyers. They can also be great sources for information not only on their own puppies, but, because of a true love of the breed as a whole, on other possibilities like rescues and adoptions.

Backyard Breeders Backyard breeders are dubious sources at best. Although it may be possible to find backyard breeders that have high-quality pedigrees, this is not the norm. These breeders frequently have litters. This makes getting a puppy from them easier, and sometimes cheaper. However, it cannot be overstated that before any such purchase you should fully check into the puppy's pedigree for health and longevity. Some breeders will have

CAUTION

Breeder Warning Signs

It is not always easy to know when you are dealing with a breeder of questionable practices, but here are a few things that should raise warning flags:

- Breeders who are reluctant to let you meet the parents or have little information about them.
- Breeders who have "papers" on their sires or dams but not pedigrees.
- Breeders who are selling a dog for "someone else."
- Breeders who publicize that they offer and breed "rare" colors.
- Breeders who offer "rare" or "exotic" breeds (actually mutts) for high prices.
- Breeders with sires and/or dams who are unregistered or registered with an unrecognized club.

CHECKLIST

Questions to Ask the Breeder

When considering a breeder, be sure to check the following.

✔ How long have they been breeding? Though one should not dismiss a new breeder, experienced breeders can offer a confidence and comfort level for the first-time buyer.

✔ Where can you see the puppy? Just remember, a breeder's home is not a petting zoo. They may not be open for visits all the time for various reasons. For example, if they have a new litter, they may restrict outside visitors for health reasons. They may wish to screen buyers by meeting them first at a neutral location. Ask to see the parents (at least the dam) and siblings (if they have any). Both are good insights into your potential puppy.

✔ Is the pedigree available? Every serious breeder will have pedigrees available either at home or on their website. Most are simple lists of the parentage. Some have photos.

✔ What are the conditions of the sale? Responsible breeders will have a standard contract outlining things like sale requirements, registration of the puppy, possible health guarantees (usually 48 hours to seven days), expectations, and such. Note if there is any wording on how disputes may be handled. (Some breeders will insist upon the return of the puppy.)

✔ How do you pay? Most breeders will accept only cash or money order. Some may take credit cards or online payments.

✔ When can I get my puppy? It is best that puppies not leave their litter until at least 8 weeks of age. Any earlier deprives the puppy of essential learning and bonding time with its canine family. After 12 weeks, a puppy may have some initial trouble adjusting to his new home, but given love, security, and routine he should do fine.

found one dog of quality and simply bred it to whatever dog they found, with little thought other than money.

There are many horror stories of people who have purchased a puppy from such breeders only to have their beloved pet develop temperament issues or a serious health problem in a matter of months. The breeder will often disregard the problem and may drop completely out of contact. Sometimes the problem requires expensive medical procedures. Sometimes there is nothing medicine can do and the puppy lives a tragically short life.

Puppy Mills Puppy mills are where dogs are considered livestock. Breeding dogs is just a matter of profit. There is no reason for anyone to ever consider purchasing a puppy from a mill. Information is plentiful on the problems involved with getting such a puppy. These operations exist because there is always someone in too big a hurry to wait for a proper breeder. If you care about dogs, do not allow these businesses to continue, as they truly do not have the dogs' best interest at heart. Luckily Great Danes are of a size that most puppy mills choose not to breed them, as space and upkeep is more than they wish to handle.

A Good Breeder Will Care

Generally, a good breeder is more interested in placing a puppy in a proper home than simply making a sale. They will ask you as many questions as you ask them. A Great Dane breeder should ask about your history with large dogs, and whether your household is ready for such a challenge. They may have a questionnaire asking for information on veterinary references, history of previous pets, style of house, type of jobs, size of your family, and such. The care a breeder shows in finding a good home is one sign of the care a breeder shows in all aspects of the breeding process.

Rescue

Another way to gain a Dane is to rescue one. First-time owners can be overwhelmed by the final size a Great Dane can reach and seek a new home for him. Then there are the unfortunate circumstances that make it financially difficult to keep a giant breed healthy and fed. Fortunately, there are a number of rescue organizations that help place such dogs.

Breed Needs

Why Adopt an Adult?

The joys of a puppy in the house are well known. Some may wonder why one would choose to adopt an adult Great Dane. There are a number of good reasons to do so.

- Adults can sometimes be less expensive, having already gone through all the costs of puppy vaccines. Be aware, though, that you may have medical costs associated with older dogs.
- Many adult dogs have already been through some housetraining and obedience so may need less training.
- An adult can sometimes help in raising younger dogs you may have.

A rescue Great Dane can be the perfect introduction of the breed to your home. But sadly, not all rescue organizations are equal. A rescue organization should not demand money upfront to visit their dogs. They should also not demand that you accept one of their dogs if you visit. A responsible rescue will schedule an interview with prospective adoptees. They may ask for previous pet information, veterinary records, and such. Many will even do home checks. Most rescues will require an adoption fee should you choose to add one of their charges to your family. Not only does this monetary amount pay for the dog and health care it has received, but it may help other Great Danes in need.

Rescue organizations can be a great source for a companion Great Dane, especially when adopting an adult, as you may bypass puppy issues like housebreaking and teething. However, because the past of most rescue dogs is unknown, one can never be certain of personality issues involved and possible baggage they may harbor. Some rescues place their charges in foster homes where temporary families get to know the dog. These homes share this information with potential permanent adopters. Given time, care, and proper training, most rescued Great Danes can become wonderful and loving family members.

Your First Look at a Puppy

Many people wanting a new dog want to start with a puppy. Once you think you have found the one for you, take some time to be sure it will be the Great Dane to share your life with.

It truly is a small world, and one can acquire their Great Dane from literally any corner of the globe. Though no amount of photos, videos, or descriptions can take the place of actually meeting and interacting with a puppy in person, sometimes one has to make decisions based on whatever information is available and gut feelings.

If possible, meeting the puppy in person is always the best option. This gives you the chance to handle the puppy. Also try to bring as many family members as may be dealing with the puppy. It lets the puppy see your

BE PREPARED Puppies Are Individuals

No matter where one gets a puppy, it must be remembered that puppies are living beings. Breeders, professional and hobby, will strive to produce healthy puppies. However, that said, like any living being, whether person or pet, there can always be health ailments and issues. A breeder is not God.

Good breeders research their lines and choose what direction for breeding they feel is best. But even parents that may have passed all known health clearances on hips, eyes, heart, thyroid, and so on can still produce offspring with health problems or show faults. A good breeder will be there for support through the good and bad.

family, and allows you to view how your family will handle a new puppy. For example does any of your family seem nervous or frightened around the puppy? And does anyone seem repulsed by the hair, slobber, and so on? These could be signs that not all members are ready yet.

Use the time with the puppy for more than just play; use it to take a good look at the pup. Are the eyes bright, not cloudy? Is the nose moist but not runny? Is the skin and coat soft without bumps, scabs, parasites, and so on? Are there any odd lumps or bumps on his body? Sniff him for any signs of foulness or odor. Check under his tail for signs of diarrhea or irritation. Is breathing normal and movement coordinated? (Being a puppy, he will tend to stumble a bit as he is still learning where his feet are.) These are simple ways to gauge general health. If anything seems odd, be sure to ask the breeder. They should be able to answer any concerns.

But even the best of eyes cannot see what the future holds for a puppy's health and temperament. Certainly, there are visual clues that you can catch from a personal visit, but there may be issues inside that cannot be seen. You might ask about tests for hip dysplasia and heart problems. Though some-times occurring at young ages, these are health issues that usually appear later in life—so be sure to ask about the parents' health.

Health Tests

When talking with breeders, you may be told about a variety of health screenings the parents and possibly the puppies have had. Some of the common tests are listed here.

OFA—The Orthopedic Foundation for Animals evaluates hip X rays for signs of canine hip dysplasia (CHD), a common bone disorder of larger breeds. By examining a single X ray the OFA will rate the dog's hips for formation of the ball and hip joint. If it passes, it will be rated from excellent to fair. Although this is useful information, the rating does not guarantee your Great Dane will or will not get CHD. (For more on this see Chapter 6.)

Pennhip—A not-for-profit program of the University of Pennsylvania uses several images to check hips for ball and hip joint formation as well as the laxity (looseness) of it. They then rate with a percentage against others of its breed.

CERF—The Canine Eye Registration Foundation offers a noninvasive eye test for possible heritable eye disease. This test can be done on puppies as young as seven weeks of age. As eyes can change with age, the certification is good for 12 months from the date of the exam.

Thyroid—Tests for normal function or autoimmune thyroiditis or idiopathic Hypothyroidism. Abnormal thyroids can cause fatigue, anemia, hair loss, mood swings, cold intolerance, high cholesterol, slow heart rate, weight gain, mental dullness, and lethargy.

There is also a CHIC number. The Canine Health Information Center (CHIC) is a database sponsored by the AKC and the OFA. The CHIC number is given to a dog when breed-specific tests are administered and the results made public. No matter what the results are, the dog will receive a CHIC number. Tests for the Great Dane are as follows:

- Hips—either OFA or Pennhip
- Thyroid—can be given at 12 months, and is recommended every two years
- Eyes—CERF
- Heart—checking for heart murmurs (unusual or extra heart sounds), which may indicate defects or disease

Again, all of these tests are valid only for the dog tested at the time of the test. They are no guarantee of future health, or the health of any offspring.

Ask if the puppy has had any medical attention to date. Puppies may have received a clean bill of health checkup by a veterinarian and possibly vaccinations. (See Chapter 4 for more on vaccines.) He may have had his dewclaws removed. (These are the claws on the front legs below the wrists.) Some veterinarians or breeders will give de-wormer to puppies as a preventive measure. If any of these have occurred, the breeder should have the medical records or at least receipts. Note that not all breeders believe in such medical practices at an early age.

Your brain may tell you not to be influenced by the cute wriggling body, wagging tail, happy licks, and warm puppy breath in your embrace. But your heart will feel the ageless desire to coddle and care for such a young, helpless soul. That is why, if possible, you should try not to be in a situation where you must decide upon the first visit if a specific puppy is to be a new family member. It is not a bad thing to think it over; after all, this is a life-altering decision not only for you and your family but for the Great Dane puppy as well.

The Mind of the Puppy

Equal to physical health, mental health is a vitally important aspect of your puppy. Personality and temperament are essential elements that will shape how you and your puppy get along. Puppies, like people, can have varied personalities. Some may take after a parent. Some may be similar to a sibling. It is even possible for each puppy in a litter to have a distinctly different personality. So the more you can discover about your potential puppy's personality, the better.

When evaluating puppies in a litter, there are some signs of potential personality "problems" even at a young age. Early signs of aggression or fear issues can be seen in puppies that growl or snap at others. Puppies that

cringe or urinate when picked up may indicate early fear issues. Although it is possible that the puppy will grow out of these traits, they can be a reflection of what the adult dog will be like.

Puppies in a litter do not grow and develop at the same rate. They may not all have similar energy, depending on when they played last. Also, they will already be starting to develop a rank amongst themselves, so you may note that some puppies seem to be dominant over others. Some simple growls and snaps at each other is nothing to be overly concerned about.

Finally, be sure to talk with the breeder. A responsible breeder will have had time to follow the growth of the litter and see traits develop. They will be able to help guide you to a puppy that may be more suited to your needs and lifestyle. For example, they may note which ones are more "dog oriented" (a bit more independent) and which are more "people oriented" (ones who seems to desire human companionship), and which ones seem to have a higher energy level.

Puppy Aptitude Tests

Although a puppy aptitude test can give you a hint of how a puppy rates next to its littermate, no test is perfect. Every puppy's environment will be different, and once in a new home, he may begin to develop differently based on his living conditions and family. Again, such tests are simply tools to help you decide if a puppy may be ideal for you.

FYI: Show Titles

Some breeders will make a lot of noise about show titles of the parents, grand-parents, and such. Like so many other factors, having a Champion for a parent does not mean your puppy will become a Champion.

But a breeder who talks of titles in their bloodline does show that they are attempting to maintain the breed standard. (The standard can be found in Chapter 10.)

This is not to say that dogs without titles will produce less standard puppies. There can be a variety of reasons dogs at shows do not win titles, and none may be because of the quality of the dog. (More on this in Chapter 7.) Most responsible breeders work very hard to create puppies of good quality with the possibility of going into the ring and winning.

It must also be remembered that not all titles come before a name. Although a title in conformation (from competition), such as Champion or Grand Champion, precedes a name, a great variety of titles ranging from agility to obedience come after the name. These post-name titles, which often refer to skills and talents, should not be overlooked and often indicate a well-balanced dog.

Puppy aptitude tests were developed to identify potential guide and service dogs. The tests are usually performed at around 49 days (seven weeks). The tester is ideally someone with whom the puppies are not familiar.

You can actually perform the same tests when you meet any potential puppy. Here are some of the steps:

- Try to get the puppy to come to you. A puppy that comes to you quickly indicates a puppy that is generally more social than independent.
- Gently roll the puppy onto his back. A puppy that struggles may be more dominant as an adult.
- Step a few feet away and make a loud clap or other sharp sound. The puppy may bark or look at you. This test is also good simply to check the puppy's hearing ability. (This is very important, as Great Danes that are primarily white may be deaf.)
- Put a towel or handkerchief in sight of the puppy, and then jerk it away to one side. A puppy that follows the object with his eyes is showing good vision and alertness. Disinterest from the puppy may indicate aloofness, or even a brain that is slow to develop.
- Lift the puppy off the ground. A puppy that accepts it shows a gentler, submissive soul. A struggling puppy may indicate a desire to dominate the pack.
- Walk away from the puppy. If he follows readily, he more likely will continue to be a follower and eager pack member as an adult. A puppy that simply sits may be less interested in socializing.

Chapter Four

Caring for a Great Dane Puppy

Adding a puppy to your lives can be a time the whole family enjoys and remembers. To make certain the experience remains positive and enjoyable, here is information that will prepare you for the joys and challenges ahead and make life with your Great Dane the best possible.

Growing a Great Dane

A Great Dane will do most of his growing in the first year. The most obvious growth will be in the area of height and weight. It is possible for a Great Dane to grow as much as an inch in one day! But the average new owner can expect to see his puppy gain 2 to 3 inches a week. Not as easily seen are the changes happening inside him as his brain and hormones mature. As he grows, his needs (physically, emotionally, nutritionally) will change, as will your role as companion.

Dogs, like people, grow at different rates. Even Great Dane littermates can have different growth charts, emotional changes, and social skill developments. Although some puppy guide charts offer day-to-day or week-to-week development, these guides should not be taken as the authority on how your own Great Dane will grow.

Before your puppy arrives home (ideally no younger than eight weeks of age), he has already had a great amount of change in his short life. His eyes and ears have opened, he has learned how to walk and play, and his needle-like baby teeth have erupted. Your puppy will have been weaned from his mother's milk and be eating solid foods. His diet will set his body up for growing, as well as begin setting his taste buds. (Studies have shown that the wider the variety of foods given to puppies in their youth, the more expansive the adult dog's palate will be.) His experiences exploring will help determine his reaction to new things. He may have discovered toys, or be totally unaware of what one does with a toy. Depending on the size of his litter and interaction with his breeder, he may begin favoring canine or human companionship, though some may seem to have a balance of both.

Your Great Dane may have even started some training exercises such as housetraining and coming when called.

When your puppy comes home, you will become the most important thing in his life. You should be aware of the basic changes that will be happening in his first six months and how to handle some of them. Below are some key events that you will want to prepare for.

Testicles Drop. If your puppy is male, both his testicles should be in his scrotum by around eight weeks of age. They can be felt, but do not worry if sometimes you can feel only one or the other, as they may yo-yo a bit in early puppyhood. As long as you can see or feel both on occasion, it is not a problem. If you cannot locate them, you may want to consult your breeder and veterinarian. Not only must two descended testicles be apparent for showing in conformation, but testicles that do not descend may cause a future medical problem.

Fear Period. At around eight weeks, your Great Dane is at the beginning of a natural fear phase, designed to keep puppies like him from leaving the protection of the den and engaging in life-threatening experiences. This period begins at eight weeks and lasts for months, depending on temperament and environment. This is a time to be cautious around your puppy. Although it is good to expose him to things in hopes of keeping his fear low, it is important to know that sudden frights can greatly affect his future years. If he is scared by a loud noise, or flash of light, or a strange sensation (such as the ground shaking), it may make him nervous about such actions or elements later in life.

Vaccinations. At one time vaccinations beginning at six weeks were considered standard. As veterinary science advances, more studies are bringing into question the best time to start vaccines, the number of vaccines, and the frequency. Consult with your breeder and veterinarian to establish a vaccination program. (See page 52.)

Adult Teeth. Starting at 12 weeks it is possible for your Great Dane to start losing his puppy teeth and having them replaced with his adult ones. This is usually a fairly simple process, with most of the puppy teeth being ingested while eating—so finding one can be a rare find. When he loses a tooth, things can get a bit bloody for some puppies. Don't be surprised to find blood around his mouth, on favorite chew items, and on parts of his body that he has mouthed. Like humans, sometimes the baby teeth will not fall out on their own. They may need some help from you or your veterinarian. Do not let baby teeth stay in too long once the adult teeth begin to show up, as it can create a variety of dental problems.

Rank. By 16 weeks of age your Great Dane will begin establishing his ranking order in the household. He will decide who is more important in the "pack," who is equal, and who is ranked lower. The most important member will be the one he pays the most attention to. Those who are his equal will be considered playmates that he does not always need to heed. Those lower in the pack are those he will not feel compelled to listen to at all. The pack will consist of all family members, humans, and other pets.

It is not unusual for a cat or small dog to be seen as higher in the pack and not to be challenged. As long as humans are always considered the alpha of the pack, there should be little chance of "disagreements" between all four-legged family members.

Rougher Play. As your Great Dane gets older, he will get rougher in play. Because of his size, this can be more of a problem than with smaller breeds. When play gets too rough, distract your puppy, or, if need be, discipline him. You may need to administer a quick nose pinch (simulating a correction his mother may have given), a tongue hold (grabbing the tongue and holding it outside of his jaw), or even a "quiet time" session. Be certain your dog knows when he is being too rough. Cue words like *"Ouch!"* or crying out *"Yipe!"* when he gets rough can help teach bite inhibition from an early age. This may help him gauge when his playing is too harsh for the rest of the family.

Chewing. Between 12 and 16 weeks of age your Great Dane should begin his chewing phase. He needs to do some chewing to help his baby teeth be expelled. A Great Dane's baby teeth are like tiny needles that can penetrate almost any cloth. His chewing behavior needs to be observed and managed. Rough chewing, as when teething, can be a good thing. At these times, wet and roll up a washcloth and then freeze it. Your young puppy can chew on the hardness while the cold temperature eases his mouth discomfort. Frozen carrots also work—but you may find carrot bits on the floor and in his stool. As your Great Dane gets older, he should be supplied with appropriate chewing articles so that he works on them and not your favorite shoes.

HOME BASICS
Puppy-Proofing Your House

- Remove or secure small objects. Small objects can be easily found and swallowed by curious puppies. Keep the floor around any puppy area picked up.
- Raise, remove, or cover electrical wires. Puppies love to chew as they begin teething. Along with damaging your items, they can chew on cords and wires that could shock them.
- Cover or block entrances and exits. Exploring puppies may not always be graceful or stable. Block any entryways to danger such as stairways, closets, fireplaces, swimming pools, fishponds, exits, and such.
- Lock away dangerous edibles. A puppy may try to eat anything it finds. Check your home for plants that may be dangerous because of poison or injury, including American holly, chrysanthemum, mistletoe, and foxglove. (A complete list of plants can be found at *www.ansci.cornell.edu/plants/dogs/index.html*.) Also secure any chemicals, medications, and cleaners.
- Keep up with growth. Great Dane puppies grow very quickly. Be certain any barriers (pens, outside fences, door gates, and so on) are high enough and properly secured.

Training. Every Great Dane needs basic obedience training whether it is done privately at home or with a professional in a class. At about three months of age, your puppy is beginning his best time period for training. This is an ideal time to introduce him to *sit, stand, stay,* and the like. Attending a training class is good for not only training but socializing your Great Dane as well. Some suggest that a dog's ability to learn begins to diminish by around the fifth month; however, unlike the old adage, you *can* teach old dogs new tricks.

Spay/Neuter. Many pet dogs get spayed or neutered at less than one year of age. Conventional wisdom said Great Danes not meant for the show ring or breeding should be spayed or neutered while young to reduce the effects of puberty (moods) and accidental pregnancies. Today, with more research being done on the subject, some are suggesting that such alterations may actually be worse for your dog's health, especially if done at a very young age. (See page 58.)

Safety First
With a puppy, you want to be sure he will be safe from accidents. To make certain that you give your puppy and family the best start, you need to be prepared even before the big day of his arrival. Key to remember is that puppies are like children. They need special attention to prevent accidents and injuries.

Housetraining

One of the most important things you can ever teach your Great Dane is to use the outside for any potty business. The sooner your pup knows where to potty, the less stress there will be in the house. He can start to be taught where to potty, aka be housebroken, as soon as he becomes aware of potty areas. Because of the size of a Great Dane, and his bladder, puppy pee pads and other such items will be of little use. Of more use will be plenty of enzyme-based urine cleansers like Nature's Miracle or Odoban.

Pups as young as five weeks of age may begin looking away from their sleeping, eating and play area (i.e., their den area) to void their bladders and bowels. This is the first sign that they recognize the need to make waste away from their living quarters. It is this desire to keep a clean house that makes a crate a big assistance in potty training. By nine weeks, he should have found certain places where he prefers to urinate and defecate.

The key to successful potty training is to be as regular as possible with your Great Dane's schedule, and observant of his movements. Generally, a puppy needs to go after he wakes up, after he eats or drinks, after he plays,

Helpful Hints

Potty Time!

Three key times when the puppy should be taken to the potty zone:

1. When the puppy wakes up
2. When the puppy finishes a meal
3. When the puppy plays

and before bedtime. Taking him out at timed intervals can help with the training too. At three months of age, he should be able to hold his urine around three hours. At four months, allow four hours. By six months, he should be able to hold it for six hours or more.

You can help your Great Dane puppy maintain a schedule through your actions. Feeding him on a regular time schedule can help him stabilize a bowel movement timetable. But be aware that feeding your puppy a constantly changing diet or too many snacks can cause temporary diarrhea. Vaccines may also affect his stool. Your Great Dane should have greater success at lasting overnight if you don't let him eat or drink a lot before bedtime.

While training, it's a good idea to find several places for him to recognize as "safe potty zones." Also, if possible, find at least two different surface textures (for example, grass and pavement). This will keep your puppy from having trouble going somewhere unfamiliar when traveling to new places that may not have what he is used to voiding upon. It is also advantageous to train your puppy to potty while on a leash, as many dogs will resist going while being held on-lead. It is times like this that a cue word during training is very helpful.

Potty-Training Methods

There are all sorts of ways suggested for potty training. A puppy-friendly and generally rapid format is for you, personally, to take your Great Dane puppy outside for the job. When you see him starting to fuss, or at a proper time, pick him up (if he is still the size to do so) and take him outside to one of the designated potty spots. Be sure to keep him focused on the task at hand. Don't let him use the time to play or explore. As he wanders, keep putting him back on the potty area. Once the deed is done, give happy praise immediately. He will catch on quickly that this is the right and good thing to do.

At this time, you can also begin training him to potty on command. This is especially useful when traveling

or doing shows. When he begins to potty, use a cue word or phrase such as "Pee pee," "Go potty," or "Better go now." Follow the task immediately with praise. He will eventually connect the cue words, the action, and the well-liked praise. Once he connects the cue word, you can begin using it before he goes, to encourage him to go.

Accidents Will Happen

Until your Great Dane puppy has enough control, and you have enough knowledge of his schedule and needs, there will be accidents. He is still developing his emotions and brain, so your reactions will directly affect his actions. Showing anger will only cause him to feel guilt and fear. These may make him wary of going potty around you, making future training difficult.

If you discover an accident after the fact, simply clean it up and note the location. Since dogs frequently potty in the same place, his return to the spot may indicate he needs to use the bathroom.

If you catch him starting, or in the act, distract him with a sharp sound like a clap or single word (too much noise could induce a fear reaction). This should cause him to pause if he can. Should he have to go very badly, he may not be able to stop. If that is the case, let him finish. You do not want him walking or running around while he finishes his business. If he can stop and is still small enough, pick him up and usher him outside. Once outside, praise him when he continues his business in the right place. Follow with some snuggling.

Your Great Dane will not be a puppy for long. After he has gotten well trained in going potty outside, you can begin to expand his household roam. Just remember to keep an eye on him, and don't be discouraged by the occasional accident.

In times you cannot be home, a crate can be a safe place for your puppy. Just be certain to leave plenty of bedding that can be washed should there be an accident. But know that having accidents too frequently can cause a setback in training.

Crates Are Great!

One of the best investments you can make for your new family member is a pet crate. A crate gives your Great Dane a secure place of his own and gives you peace of mind. Crates can aid with potty training, can provide a private eating environment, and can even become a home away from home when traveling. All dogs should be crate trained. It will also prepare your dog for any crating necessary because of stays at veterinarians, shows, or air travel.

But crates are not the answer to everything. You should never use the crate to punish your dog. Remember, it is his safe haven, not a jail. Finally, crates should never be used as holding pens for problem dogs. Dogs that must spend all of their time in a crate will develop behavioral problems caused by a lack of socialization and attention.

You will want to start your dog's relationship with his crate early. Keep the door open while he wanders the room. Put his toys inside so he will be tempted to enter it. Toss a treat in for him to get. Another good way to get your dog to think positively about his crate is to feed him in it. In no time he will associate the crate with a positive experience and a safe place. Note: When your Great Dane goes into the crate, do not immediately close the door. You do not want him to think that every time he walks into the crate, the door will slam shut behind him.

Keep increasing the time your Great Dane spends in his crate. As you expand the uses of the crate, initiate a cue word. "Crate" or "Kennel up" are good ones. Should he get anxious in the crate and begin fussing, do not let him out immediately. In the beginning, wait for him to calm to the count of three or five to be certain he is not simply taking a breath. Then open the crate and let him out. You never want to give him the impression that being loud or fussing will get him released. (You will need to be aware of the difference between general fussing and the need to potty, which may take a while to figure out.)

The crate is also the place for quiet time. All puppies need additional time to rest so that they can grow. Favorite bedding and a toy inside for them to snuggle with can make it even homier. Let all family members, especially children, know that when he is in his crate, he should be allowed to rest. Soon he will realize that the crate is for his privacy too. It should also be noted that the crate can be used to let other members of the house rest from the puppy's wild antics, even if it is for only 20 minutes or so.

To further establish the crate as a pleasant experience be sure to keep your puppy's safety in mind. No dog should wear a collar while in a crate. Collars can accidentally catch on handles and openings, possibly choking them. Although you want to make sure he has bedding in the crate, be certain any bedding or toys are of a safe nature, with no stuffing or loose ends that could be torn off, torn into, and eaten.

Be aware that with some crates small puppies may be able to stick a paw out and get it caught, causing distress in both him and you. Usually you just need to settle him and release his paw with a slight movement. Young and older dogs can possibly get a tooth caught if they mouth the wire gate (or door). Again, this will cause a great amount of noise and turmoil until you gently free the tooth. To aid in preventing this, stop the behavior when you see your Great Dane chewing at the gate (or any part of the crate). This can be done in a number of ways. Sometimes an abrupt clearing of your throat will startle him to stop. If this doesn't work, you may wish to rattle a can full of pennies or use a spray bottle with water (or water and a small bit of apple cider vinegar for scent) to distract him so that he stops.

CAUTION

Scared Puppies Can Bite

A puppy that is trapped by the foot or tooth (for example, on an ex-pen or crate) can become very scared. Although you will want to immediately set to work to untangle him, be aware that he will most likely be thrashing about and snapping his jaw. This may lead to an unintentional bite from the puppy—and since Great Dane puppies can be quite large, the bite could be sizable. If you get bitten, do not correct the puppy; instead, continue trying to soothe him, and seek treatment for your wound. Such a bite is not indicative of bad behavior on the dog's part and should not initially be considered a problem. Only if biting becomes a habit does the behavior need to be dealt with.

Early Health and Nutrition

As your Great Dane grows in size, his body will need the proper nutrition to support his, at times, rapid growth. He will also need to keep his body defenses up to combat a variety of problems, from diseases to parasites. When it comes to information on health and nutrition in dogs, the emphasis has often been more on medication than preventive health itself.

Vaccines

Before his first vaccine, your Great Dane puppy gained temporary immunity from diseases through his mother's own milk. For the first several days of nursing, a bitch's milk contains a substance known as colostrum. It is this substance that gives newborns some protection from disease. (Should you ever find yourself in need of substitute mother's milk for a newborn, always be sure that the brand you use has colostrum in it, such as Just Born.) After several weeks that immunity begins to fade.

The use of vaccines has become one of the three most debated aspects of Great Dane ownership—the other two being diet and ear cropping. Conventional wisdom used to be to vaccinate early and frequently with a variety of vaccines, starting at around the puppy's sixth week. The once-fixed schedule called for new shots every few weeks.

Today, as research and new tests expand the knowledge on vaccines, their effectiveness, and their side effects, experts are suggesting differing vaccine schedules. Even the American Animal Hospital Association and the American Veterinarian Medical Association now advocate a variety of vaccine schedules. And many medical groups no longer fully support the multiple vaccine inoculations. Talk with your breeder and veterinarian for a program best suited for your dog and his environment.

Generally the first vaccine should be given to a puppy no sooner than eight weeks. This first round is for the four classic puppy health problems:

FYI: Vaccine Types

There are two designations of vaccines: core and noncore.

Core vaccines are those recommended, and sometimes required, for boarding and participation in public events, for all dogs. These currently include rabies, distemper, parainfluenza, parvovirus, and hepatitis.

Noncore vaccines are those only suggested. They include inoculations for bordetella, Lyme disease, and leptospirosis.

Frequently Asked Questions on Vaccines per Dr. Jean Dodds

Q. Is there a risk of over-vaccinating?

A. Yes. Vaccines contain material designed to challenge the immune system of the pet, and so can cause adverse reactions. They should not be given needlessly, and should be tailored to the pet's individual needs.

Q. Is it safe to vaccinate pregnant pets?

A. Absolutely not.

Q. Should vaccines be given more often than two weeks apart even if a different vaccine is being given?

A. No. The safest and most effective interval is three to four weeks apart.

Q. Can a pet fail to develop an immune response after vaccination?

A. Yes. This is a genetic characteristic seen particularly in Great Danes. Even boosting them regularly may not produce measurable immunity.

distemper, hepatitis, parainfluenza, and parvovirus. Distemper is in the same family as human measles and can damage skin, eyes, the respiratory tract (coughing is a sign), and even the brain. Hepatitis is similar to its human counterpart, attacking the liver and kidneys. Parainfluenza is a respiratory disease causing coughing. Parvovirus attacks the intestines and can infect the heart muscle, causing sudden death. Originally this was given as a mega "DHLPP" shot. (The *L* is for leptospirosis, another disease affecting organs, but the vaccine has come under scrutiny and is not always administered. Instead a DHPP shot is administered.) Today, many veterinarians are giving inoculations as single injections over combinations. These vaccines are often repeated again at 12 and 16 weeks of age.

At 16 weeks of age the rabies vaccine is given. Rabies is a neurological disease usually transmitted through a bite from an infected animal. Because most mammals (such as squirrels, bats, and raccoons) can carry the disease, dogs in rural areas are assumed to be more at risk. Rabies is a disease that can be contracted by humans, so the time period for first vaccination is often controlled by local laws.

Once your Great Dane reaches adulthood, regular booster vaccines for several of these diseases is commonly recommended. Rabies boosters are often dictated by law.

Currently, many Great Dane authorities point to the vaccine protocol suggested by Dr. Jean Dodds. This plan has fewer vaccines given at longer intervals to allow the puppy to weather each vaccine. It also looks to the dog's buildup of natural defenses, called titers, as evidence to reduce vaccines in older dogs. (There is a growing movement to lengthen the time between rabies vaccines in adult dogs to seven years from the current every one to three years, depending on your location.) You can read more at *www.itsfortheanimals.com/DODDS-CHG-VACC-PROTOCOLS.HTM.*

De-Worming

Most breeders check and treat for worms in their litters. So most likely, by the time you get your puppy home, he will have had his first checkup and

FYI: Common Canine Worms

- **Heartworm.** One of the most publicized of canine worm problems is the heartworm. This worm is introduced through mosquito bites. The worm grows in the heart and can kill your dog. A readily available monthly treatment (not a true preventive) can be gotten from a veterinarian. Though most veterinarians require blood tests before prescribing the medication, some may begin the treatment automatically in areas where the worm is prevalent. It should be noted that the most commonly prescribed drug is ivermectin. Clinical studies have shown this drug to have serious side effects in humans and animals, which can include neurotoxicity leading to depression and loss of muscle coordination known as ataxia. Some have found success combatting heartworms holistically. (More information is available at *www.naturalrearing.com/coda/n_heartworm.html.*)
- **Tapeworms.** If you see small, flat, white segments in your dog's stool, he may have tapeworms. Tapeworm elimination requires special medication. Tapeworms are acquired when your Great Dane eats a flea, so your best prevention is flea control. Not only are there flea collars, sprays, and applications available for flea control, but many people use human-grade diatomaceous earth inside the house and outside with great success. This fine, all-natural powder causes fleas to dehydrate and die. It is safe enough to be approved by the U.S. Department of Agriculture as a feed additive.
- **Roundworms, hookworms, and whipworms** are also of concern to younger dogs. Like the worms above, all come from the ingestion of eggs. (Some of the eggs can survive years in the soil.) Signs include a potbelly, diarrhea, weight loss, and weakness. All can be diagnosed by examining feces, and are usually easily treated if caught in time.

treatment if affected. Worms are one of the most common "ailments," as they can come from a variety of sources, including the dam and things your puppy finds to ingest. This is a great reason to keep areas clean of feces. Even if he does not eat feces, his feet will pick up dirt and debris, which will enter his system when he licks himself. Luckily, most worms are easily treatable with help from your veterinarian.

Ears to you!

Great Danes, like all puppies, are born with soft, floppy drop ears. When the breed was used to hunt, the ears were cropped (cut) and made erect so the boars could not use them as handles to pull the dog down. The look became part of the standard for much of the world. But the tide has been shifting to leave the ears natural.

Around the world, cropping is less common, and there are even a number of countries in which it is illegal. Recently several states have considered bills outlawing or restricting the process. The American Veterinarian Medical Association opposes the practice. Many countries do not allow the cropping of ears at all. Even the American Kennel Club, in its official breed standard description of the Great Dane, lists natural ears before cropped.

Contrary to popular belief, uncropped ears are no more susceptible to infections than cropped ears. Research from the American Veterinary Medical Association shows that infections tend to plague breeds with specific glandular conditions. Breeds tending toward this issue include Cocker Spaniels (floppy ears) and German Shepherds (erect ears). The Great Dane was not shown to be affected either way.

However, in the United States, a large percentage of Great Dane show dogs are still cropped. Cropping is typically done before 12 weeks of age by a licensed veterinarian. It is a surgical procedure wherein roughly one half of each ear is amputated and then sutured. Proper cleaning and care must be taken so that the desired appearance of upright ears is achieved. Veterinarians with a great deal of cropping experience may be able to determine if the ear leather is itself suitable for cropping.

Whether he has natural or cropped ears, you may need to train his ears to get the proper look. (The teething period can affect the carriage of the ear.) The Great Dane Club of America standard says that ears "shall be high set, medium in size and of moderate thickness, folded forward close to the cheek. The top line of the folded ear should be level with the skull. If cropped, the ear length is in proportion to the size of the head and the ears are carried uniformly erect."

Natural ears may not naturally hang "close to the cheek." Instead they can be raised from the head, pointing outward like a wing look—sometimes called "airplane ears." To aid your dog in having a proper natural ear set, you may wish to tape them. There are a number of procedures. One is creating a strap that goes from one ear, under the chin (but not touching), and attaches to the other. A step-by-step example can be found at *www.6stardanes.com/ears.html*. With luck, you can have your dog's ears looking Great Dane standard in a few months.

Breed Truths

When Great Danes were bred to hunt wild boar, the ears were cropped very short, almost to the point of having no external ears. This was done so that the boar could not grab the dog by the ear. Today, this surgery is merely a cosmetic one. In fact, there are many countries in the world where cropping a dog's ears is illegal.

Cropped ears will require more work, and often more time. How quickly you can get your dog's ears up will depend on two key factors: the style of cut, and the ear leather itself. If the ear has been cut long, it may take more work than one that has been cut closer to the head. That is because the longer the ear, the heavier it is, and the more

strength of muscle and cartilage is needed. As for the ear leather, some dogs have a very soft, floppy ear, whereas others have thick, firm ears. A firm ear will often stand faster, but too thick and heavy an ear can cause delay as well.

Cropping is typically done before 12 weeks of age. After 12 weeks the cartilage has set and most likely the cropping will not be successful. The first aspect of getting a proper standing crop is taking care of the after-surgery needs. Depending on the age of cropping and when you pick up your puppy, he may still have his stitches. These will need to be kept clean and dry as any post-surgery area would require. Upon healing, the stitches will need to be removed. While treating these areas, try to refrain from harsh antibacterial

CAUTION

Not All Ears Are Equal

It should also be noted, that not all ear croppings result in perfectly erect ears. Because ears must not be in tapes for showing, one can go to any Great Dane show and see a variety of cropped ear positions. Sometimes one stands and the other bends in the middle, flopping out. There are times when both ears fold back into the head, looking as if they are glued flat to the skull. You can see cropped ears that do not stand at all, lying limp like triangles against the head. Some of these may be temporary where, sadly, others may not. You can even find examples where the cropping was not even and one ear clearly is taller than the other.

or drying cleansers. These will tend to dry the skin, increasing the chances of scarring. The scars will create patches of hair loss or color loss.

Next will be the process of getting the ears to stand. You will need something to hold the ears up, like a post, and something to hold the ears to the post. The posts are set inside the front part of the ear. Posts have been made from a variety of objects, from tampons to flexible ruler sections to mole foam to foam pipe coverings. Ears can be attached with a variety of medical tapes, including sports wrap and cloth tape. Many will have to be changed every few days or at least once a week. This is to prevent both infection and too much adhesion to the skin. The longer the tape has been on the ear, the more likely hair will be removed with the tape. A good guide for taping and posting cropped ears is at *www.royalsoonerdanes.com/daneearwrapping.htm.*

As mentioned, the style of the cut and skin of the ear will be major factors in how long the process will take, as well as how diligently the owner works at it. Some pups will have ears properly standing on their own as early as 4–6 months (around 6–10 weeks of taping), whereas others may take until they are 12 months old or even older before the taping is done.

Spaying and Neutering

Spaying and neutering is the act of removing reproductive capability from your Great Dane. This is probably one of the most common of canine surgeries and is recommended for a variety of reasons ranging from mood corrections to population control. Recently this procedure has become the center of a great amount of debate from medical and political pundits.

The spaying of a bitch consists of removing her ovaries and uterus. The advantages of spaying bitches include reducing the risk of mammary (breast) tumors, eliminating the risk of pyometra (a potentially lethal infection of the uterus), and reducing the risk of perianal fistulas (infectious lesions around the anus, usually found in males). Medical data reveals a negative side to the operation, including increasing the risk for hypothyroidism, incontinence, obesity, and vaginitis among others. It may also increase the risk of adverse reactions to vaccines.

The neutering of a dog consists of removing his testes. Some believe neutering at a young age can curb aggression and leg-lifting urination (to mark

CAUTION

Danes in Heat

Beginning as early as eight months of age female Great Danes can begin having heat cycles. Officially called estrus, heat cycles last around three weeks. Symptoms of a female in heat include moodiness, bloody discharge from her uterus, and an increase in urinating (to leave her scent). Some may put britches on their female during the heat cycle to protect furnishings and carpets from the discharge. During this time, male dogs (intact or not) may show signs of panting, whining, drooling, shaking, and clawing. In fact, males have been known to knock down doors to get to a bitch in heat.

FYI: Special Interest Groups and the Government

There has been a growing movement in the United States toward mandatory spaying and neutering. Some behind this movement may have noble intentions of reducing pet populations in shelters, though there is no research to show such a cause and effect. The fact is that such a request is equal to calling for the extinction of dogs. If all domestic dogs except a few show dogs are sterilized, there will be no puppies created for future owners except perhaps for the very wealthy.

territory), but no medical research backs these assumptions. Although some point to various studies connecting neutering with behavior, others believe the behavior changes could also be caused by training or environment.

Some positive effects found include the total elimination of testicular cancer, reducing the risk of noncancerous prostate disorders, reducing the risk of perianal fistulas (lesions on the anus), and possibly reducing the risk of diabetes. But medical data suggests that negative effects include increasing risk of bone cancer, obesity, prostate cancer, cardiac hemorrhaging, hip dysplasia, and other serious considerations. The pros and cons of this surgery should be weighed seriously by every owner.

The time to alter a dog is one of the most hotly contested issues in the debate. While state and local governments attempt to lower the age for spaying and neutering through legislation (some to as young as four months), more and more medical research suggests delaying the operation to at least one year. Altering a dog too early can affect his overall growth. The loss of essential hormones in the testes can slow the bone's growth plate closure, creating a tall and lanky dog that may have future bone problems. (See Chapter 10.)

It is important to remember that with any surgery there are risks. There

Helpful Hints

1. When choosing a veterinarian, make sure that he or she has experience and the proper testing equipment for giant breeds.
2. Know that holistic health and preventive health are becoming more accepted in medical journals. You can find a holistic veterinarian near you by going to the American Holistic Veterinary Association's site: http://www.ahvma.org/.
3. Because medical expenses are constantly increasing, and a Great Dane often requires human-sized doses of medications, you may wish to consider health insurance for your pet. There are several options in health insurance today specifically tailored to your Great Dane's lifestyle.

is the chance of adverse reactions to the anesthesia, subsequent inflammation, and infection. An occasional dog can be allergic to anesthesia as well
as sutures. These concerns are even stronger in younger Great Danes. One
should remember that at around five months of age, your Great Dane is
equal in age to a six-year-old child. Putting one so young through such an
extreme procedure, although well intentioned, may not be in your dog's best
interest. Many Great Dane enthusiasts wait until at least 18 months before
neutering and hold off on spaying bitches until just before their first heat. If
your Great Dane requires surgery for any reason, a recommended protocol
for anesthesia has been developed by the Great Dane Club of America and is
available on its website at *www.gdca.org.*

Puppy Nutrition

As your Great Dane gets bigger, his body will need the proper nutrition
to support his, at times, rapid growth. The fact is that puppies will eat just
about anything. It is up to you to guide your Great Dane to a nutritious diet
that will help him live a long and healthy life.

More than ever there are an enormous number of food options available
for your Great Dane. As with food for humans, not all choices are the most
healthful. Because of serious pet food scares, today's pet food producers are
more conscious of their ingredients. Before deciding on a diet, talk with your
breeder. They should be familiar with the breed and the specific bloodline
of your puppy. A more complete discussion of food and nutrition is in the
"Health and Nutrition" chapter on page 85.

Once you have chosen your food path, your young Great Dane should be
fed at least three times a day. When he starts to regularly dismiss lunchtime,
it may be time to cut his meals down to twice a day. This is often before
eight months of age. You can add snacks, but do not let him get fat. A growing Great Dane should be on the lean side, but not skinny. One should be

able to see the hints of his back two ribs and hips.

Bone Growth Diseases

Great Dane puppies, because of their rapid growth, are especially susceptible to three bone diseases: panosteitis, hypertrophic osteo-dystrophy, and osteochrondritis dissecans.

Panosteitis, also referred to as pano or "growing pains," is perhaps the best known, the least problem-atic, and perhaps the most common of the three. Pano typically affects Great Danes between 9 and 14 months of age, but can afflict a puppy as young as 6 months of age. Symptoms of pano include limb soreness, rapid growth, and sudden lameness, which can switch from one leg to another.

The cause for panosteitis is unknown, but the outcome is usu-ally not serious. It is a self-limiting disease, meaning most puppies will grow out of it. However, before just assuming your Great Dane has pano when he limps, consult your veteri-narian to rule out other problems, which may be more serious.

Hypertrophic osteodystrophy, also known as HOD, is a bone dis-ease caused by dietary problems. It often affects rapidly growing Great

Giant Breeds and Protein

Your Great Dane will achieve his ultimate size in time. Rushing the process can be dangerous to your Great Dane's long-term health. Too many calories and too much protein can cause growth problems. Many commercial puppy foods are too high in protein for giant breeds. It is best to feed a high-quality dry food with a dry matter protein percentage of 24 percent or less. Key to remember is that protein percent-ages on dry food are often "crude protein" and could be meat or vegetable. Most raw meats are only 14–17 percent protein because of the water in them.

To convert canned protein to dry, check the ingredients. Look at the moisture percentage and the protein percentage. Remove the moisture percentage for solid percentage. For example, a can with 75 percent moisture means 25 percent solid. Take the protein percentage on the can (say, 10) and divide it by the solid percent-age. In this case the dry protein would be 10/25, which equals 40 percent.

Also, too many calories can create an overweight youngster. Extra weight can cause a variety of health problems.

Danes between the ages of 10 weeks and 6 months. Symptoms may include large knotty joints, easty-westy feet (toes pointing inward or outward), a roached (arched) back, and a pinched (crouching) rear end. In more severe cases symptoms can include high fever, lack of appetite, sore and heated joints, decreased mobility, the flattening of feet, and the bowing of limbs.

The disease is usually caused by the consumption of too many calories versus energy used. This isn't necessarily from overfeeding; it could be an inappropriate diet for this particular puppy. The diet could be unbalan in its calcium/phosphorus ratios caused by giving too much human fo or other supplements or lacking in vital trace minerals. Even lack of vi C is considered a culprit.

If HOD is suspected, it is important to seek a veterinarian with experience in this matter. A diagnosis of HOD is often confirmed with X rays. The disease can create a high fever. If not treated, HOD can lead to permanent structural damage and even death.

Osteochrondritis dissecans (OCD) is the degeneration of cartilage that typically affects rapidly-growing Great Danes under a year of age. With this disease, cartilage cells do not develop into mature bone as they should, resulting in areas (shoulder, hocks, and stifles) with a buildup of cartilage. These areas become painfully inflamed. Symptoms include lameness and pain upon flexing the affected joint (can be more than one). The disease can be caused by an imbalance of minerals or from excessive calcium. For this reason alone it is not ideal to give Great Danes calcium supplements. If OCD is suspected, seek a veterinarian with experience in this matter.

Socialization

Socialization is perhaps the most important aspect of your Great Dane's development. Unfortunately, it is also one that is skipped by too many owners. The goal of socialization is to prepare your dog for as many of life's experiences as possible. The more positive experiences he has, the less the negative ones may affect him.

Great Dane puppies can begin life as fearless, timid, reckless, and cautious. But as they grow, even the bravest puppy can develop fears about its surround-

---

BE PREPARED! Home Alone

Great Danes are particularly social animals that enjoy company and can develop strong attachments to their family. In fact, when you are not around, they can become quite anxious and may show extreme signs of separation anxiety.

Actually, all puppies are not left alone easily. While in the care of his dam, a lonely pup will cry until she returns. Once he is in your home, he may cry when he feels he is alone, and he can cry for quite some time. You may wish to go and comfort him, but do not let this become a habit or he will continue to cry as an adult for attention. Better still is if you don't let him get away with it in the beginning.

When crying occurs, try a little distraction via a toy or sound. If you cannot always be there, a piece of clothing you have worn and not washed (like a shirt) may make a soothing bed buddy for him. Just be certain the shirt cannot be easily torn and ingested . . . and that it is not a shirt you want to keep, as it may get soiled and chewed upon.

Soft toys can also help. Often a puppy will find a favorite toy that entertains and comforts him. Some Great Danes will keep that toy as they grow older and continue to see it as a comfort factor. Such toys can be useful in times of stress and travel and help relieve some of the separation anxiety caused by your leaving.

ings and new experiences. Such fears, once established, are not easily reversed. It is in your and his best interest to begin a balanced socialization process.

One way to give positive socialization is to control your dog's earliest adventures. In the beginning you can help your Great Dane simply by introducing him to different floorings, stairs, car rides, and things he'll be doing later in life. You will want him to meet people in comfortable surroundings. A good way is to invite friends over. When out in public, be willing to ask people if they will approach your dog and greet him, but with an adorable Great Dane puppy you probably will not need to ask. You can even let him meet other sociable pets you may encounter. (But it's a good idea to have greeted the pet first to confirm its meet-ability.)

Communicating with Your Great Dane

Touch Most Great Danes enjoy being touched and petted, and yours may bump you and shove his head under your arm to remind you of your duties. Touch is the first sense nurtured as a puppy. A mother will nuzzle the newborn, licking and sniffing at him. Heat sensors in a puppy's nose allow him to find his mother and littermates. Touching between a puppy and his mother and littermates is an important part of development. Puppies not permitted such physical contact may grow into dogs with problems being handled or feeling uncomfortable when touched. If you like hugging your Great Dane, you should expose him to hugging slowly, while he is young, so that he realizes it is a sign of affection. When working on hugging, be sure to talk to your dog in a reassuring tone so he knows this is not a dominant or attack issue. Some Great Danes may wrap a front leg around you and tuck their head in against you as if to hug back. They may even enjoy having their cheeks kissed at this time.

Body Posture Most of the time your Great Dane will be in a normal posture. His body will appear relaxed with no real strain or stress evident. When dominance is needed, he will often appear to look taller by standing more straight, raising his back slightly, and holding his head high. If submissive or frightened he will try to look smaller with tucked tail, lowered head, and slightly buckled legs. When training your Great Dane, you should always be standing straight up. Slouching, shuffling, and a quiet voice may indicate that you are simply playing or only making a request. You want him to pay attention and know you are in control.

Eyes Animals use their eyes to indicate dominance, submission, and more. Never stare at any animal. Staring without moving or blinking is considered a direct challenge or threat, especially by dogs not yet familiar with you. It can create anxiety or aggression, so it is best never to stare at him when you are angry or demanding something. Try to keep a relaxed expression on your face and your eyes moving from his, to points on his head, and elsewhere. On the other hand, do not become alarmed if he stares at you. Many dogs will look at humans as a way to get their attention. If his facial expression is relaxed, he is simply showing his enjoyment of your company. Should his facial expression be tense, he may be showing signs of aggression. Slowly look away or yawn to calm him. (If this does not help, you may need to consider taking control—see page 101.)

Ears Whether natural or cropped, when he is feeling fine, his ears will look normal and relaxed. Should they begin to fold back, take note. Slightly back means he is feeling friendly toward you. When they are flat on his head, he is showing fear or submission. Try to calm him with gentle words, or distract him with a toy or treat.

Tail

Just because a dog wags his tail, it does not mean he is happy. He can wag his tail to show pleasure or even aggression. A lowered tail shows submission or fear, and his attempt to look smaller. A tail that is raised shows attention and interest. When talking to him, a slightly raised tail most likely means he is paying attention to you.

Chapter Five

Living with a Great Dane

Life with your Great Dane will most likely be a life of surprises. Like any member of your family, his personality will continue to grow and develop through his lifetime. Your Great Dane gets his basic personality from many elements: parents, early days, canine family, and even his distant ancestor, the wolf. Once he becomes yours, his actions should adapt to your family's routines and rules. But he may need a little help.

Shopping for Your Great Dane

As your Great Dane matures, you may find shopping for him to be a challenge. Many of today's pet manufacturers consider "big" or "large" to mean a dog of 50–70 pounds. That is only a fraction of what your boy weighs!

Whether shopping in person or online, look for items that are marked "giant" size. Pay special attention to the actual physical dimensions listed. Beds measuring 24 by 36 inches may be big for some breeds, but your boy will find his feet, tail, and head lying over the edge. Similarly, many blankets and clothing items will hardly cover the bare necessities of a Great Dane. When shopping for beds or bedding, you will want one dimension to be no less than 48 inches.

Keep in mind that an adult Great Dane is very close to the size of a human. Human-sized furniture, such as beds and bedding, will fit him fine. Garage sales and thrift stores are great places to pick up blankets and sheets for him. Just be cautious of blankets with stuffing or batting. Once torn or worn, the stuffing could become ingested and create a medical situation.

Also consider his size when buying toys. The strength of his jaws will demand toys that are sturdy. As to the type of toys, his personality will determine that. Some enjoy the squeakers, others the hard rubber chewable style. And despite his enormous size, he may enjoy little plush toys, but be aware that he could swallow them. You may have to go through several types of toys to find the ones that fit him. And you may discover that as he ages, his tastes change—just as humans' do.

Collaring Your Great Dane

A major part of living with a Great Dane is having him properly attired. And one of the most important pieces of "clothing" he will have is his collar. There are a wide variety of collar types available. You may need to try a few before you find the one that fits both your styles. Here are the most common collar types.

Buckle Collar. This classic collar, which fastens with a buckle, can be either flat, resembling a belt, or tubular in design. (The rolled leather can help prevent chaffing and hair loss.) The buckle collar is ideal for hanging identification tags, rabies tags, and other information such as a microchip notification. Buckle collars are good for walking or as a handle to hold your dog with. The biggest drawback may be difficulty in removing it quickly during an emergency.

Adjustable Quick-Release Collar. These collars typically have two plastic ends. One end fits into the other, creating a "snap" noise – hence they are sometimes referred to as snap collars. These collars are quick and easy on and off, and their adjustable-length feature can be a benefit with a growing Great Dane. However, the clasp may come undone should your Great Dane push his weight against it.

Break-Away Collar. Similar to the quick-release-collar, this one is specifically designed to unfasten if a strong tug is applied. However, it is designed to not unfasten when used with a leash. This collar is ideal when your Great Dane is around other dogs, as it prevents him from being choked should a dog's jaws or teeth get caught in his collar. This collar should not be used as a quick grab handle to restrain your Great Dane, as it can unfasten and release him.

Slip Collar. This is the standard collar worn by dogs in conformation showing, as they are not bulky or detracting. It is a single strand with O-shaped rings on each end. It may be crafted out of nylon, cotton, braided leather, or serpentine metal chain. Pulling the body of the collar through one O-ring creates a letter P shape. The leash is then clipped to the ring at the bottom of the P, allowing the collar to be tightened or relaxed. If the leash clip is attached to the opposite ring, the collar does not tighten.

Since this collar must go over your Great Dane's head, sizing is important. For a growing puppy, you will need to keep replacing the current collar with a larger size. Do not leave this collar on your unsupervised Great Dane, as he may catch the ring on something and choke himself.

Metal Training or Chain Collar. Often referred to as a "choke chain" this is the most often used and misused collar. Crafted out of links of metal with an O-shaped ring on each end, it is similar to the slip collar mentioned above. A pull on the leash will tighten the collar around the dog's neck. Used properly, with a quick tug, it can remind your Great Dane that he is being handled. If used poorly, it can actually choke him. This collar, when used incorrectly, can cause damage to the neck and trachea.

Prong or Pinch Collar. One of the most misunderstood of all the collars, this collar is crafted out of metal with multiple removable and replaceable sections (for sizing). Each section has two raised fingers or prongs. When used correctly, it applies pressure against the Great Dane's neck much like teeth. This gives a "pinch" effect, but should not choke the dog. The drawback is that this collar looks more menacing than the choke chain. It is actually more humane, as it should not cause neck, back, or trachea injuries like the choke chain. (Professional assistance should be given to those without experience with prong collars for proper fitting.) For those who wish to minimize the menacing appearance of a prong collar, there are decorative collar covers available.

Head Halter. Similar to a halter seen on a horse, this item is placed over the dog's head and face. The device allows full range of jaw movement so your dog can pant, drink, eat, and bark while wearing it. Since the nose band sits near the Great Dane's eyes, many will dislike how it feels and may paw at it, trying to remove it. As with any training tool, it needs to be used properly and without pulling. Constant pulling can create injuries in the neck and back. The biggest drawback is that some people will confuse the appearance of a head halter with a muzzle and may think your dog is aggressive.

CAUTION

Whenever you have gotten a new style of toy for your Great Dane, watch him play with it. Toys can become dangerous if ingested. Does he rip apart plush toys and eat the stuffing? Consider the newer line of stuffing-free toys. Does he tear off pieces of a soft rubber toy? Try the hard rubber brands.

Harness. This device is worn around the torso, leaving the head and neck free. The harness can be ideal for Great Danes who have physical restrictions or are recovering from an injury that could put undue strain on his head and neck. Before using a harness, be certain your Great Dane is well trained on a leash. The harness is an effective means of weight distribution that may allow dogs to pull and or drag many times their own weight—including you.

Shock or Remote Collars. These collars are used for specific training or correction. They have a remote device that gives a correction to the dog wearing the collar. The device can emit an electric shock or a high-pitched audio signal warning. You control the correction with a remote control. As with any electronic device, these collars will need a steady supply of batteries. These can be useful in training, but should not be overused. Always seek professional assistance before using any remote collars on your dog.

Vibrating Collars. These are standard buckle collars with a device attached that vibrates when you trigger their remote control. A vibrating collar is often used on Great Danes with hearing loss or deafness. The vibrations attract your dog's attention. The device will not cause injury, but the vibrating may initially upset some sensitive dogs. The range of the collar is usually small, making it important that your dog stays near you. As with the shock/remote collar, you will need plenty of batteries.

Talking the (Great Dane) Talk

Although it is nice (and a necessity) for your Great Dane to come when he is called, real communication is more than simple name recognition. He needs to understand what is expected of him. And you must know when he has needs. The best way to communicate is to remember how dogs speak to each other.

Think when you talk to your Great Dane. Are your words saying one thing while your body language, pitch, and tone relay something different? Dogs have a complex language of body signals and vocalizations. Base your actions on their understandings and you will be on the path to mutual communication.

The Mouth of a Great Dane

Great Danes have big mouths. (It comes with the large head.) And living with a big mouth can be trying at times. Essentially, there are three aspects of his mouth that will need your attention: his bark, his bite, and his tongue.

His bark Great Danes are big dogs, and thus can have a big bark. His bark will be loud enough to be heard a good distance away, and probably shock those standing close by. Barking is natural for dogs, and though Great Danes are not known as barkers, he will vocalize. He could be barking to sound an alarm (at a strange noise), to show excitement (over dinner), to express anger (over your being away), and even to show joy (over your

FYI: Verbal Commands

Just as with human communication, it is not what you say; it's how you say it.

- Be consistent in the words you use and the way you use them. Dogs often hear the sounds more than the words. Using different words for the same command, or different inflections, may create confusion in his mind.
- Make sure he responds on first command. Repeating a command over and over may give him the impression that he does not need to obey the first.
- Teach commands in a normal voice. Shouting commands will not make him react any more quickly. Shouting can display anger or aggression and could unsettle a sensitive Great Dane. Should he be deaf or hard of hearing, as many whites can be, you may want to train with hand signals. Hand signals are also useful to hearing dogs in situations where there is a great deal of ambient noise and times where speaking aloud may not be appropriate.
- Use the proper pitch. Low pitches, which sound like growls to a dog, are good to make him stop an action. These show power and leadership, and are a bit "threatening." High pitches, which are like puppy squeals, create a playful atmosphere and may encourage him to be more active and social. A monotone voice can be calming when he is overly excited.
- Abrupt speech and low-pitched tones will sound like a bark and attract his attention. This is why many commands are short, one-syllable words such as *Come, Sit, Down, Stay, Heel.*

arrival or about toys). To stop occasional barking, try to locate the source and then follow these steps:

1. First, do not simply shout at the dog. This will often encourage him to continue, as he will think you are barking too. The better reaction is to distract him. Clap your hands. Shake a can of coins.
2. Once he is quiet, reward him with praise or possibly a treat. You may also want to use a clicker here to bridge what the dog is doing right to receive the reward. Gradually increase the time he has to be quiet to receive a treat.
3. Always add a cue word. Avoid a common word or phrase like "quiet" or "shutup." Cue words should be somewhat unusual. Try "settle" or "hush."

Never confuse occasional barking at strange noises or actions with problem barking. A problem barker is not a dog that barks, but a dog that barks and barks and barks. Problem barkers seem to bark at everything and nothing and do not want to stop barking once started. Constant barking is a habit that is serious and needs attention.

Most problem barking comes from three situations: boredom, distress, and aggression. Boredom or a need for attention is the most common. Great Danes that are left alone with no stimulus will often bark. Toys may help alleviate boredom and reduce barking. Another common suggestion is to tire him out with activities so he will rest. Of course, puppies under one year of age will bounce back very quickly from activity.

Distress or anxiety barking occurs if a Great Dane becomes highly attached to an individual, and panics when that person leaves. This is actually a form of separation anxiety. (See page 75.) Along with barking, he may drool, pant, and even try to escape. It is almost impossible to stop distress barking alone. The problem of separation anxiety must first be controlled.

Aggressive barking occurs when a dog becomes agitated by people or animals arriving and causing him to go on the offensive, barking and lunging. Aggressive barking is frequently caused by lack of socialization as a puppy or sometimes dominance. This barking can be addressed only with socialization and training. It should be noted that the longer a Great Dane has not been socialized and worked with, the longer it may take to settle him. But with patience and time, it can be done.

His bite One of the most common questions asked of dog owners is "Does your dog bite?" A good answer would be, "Anything with a mouth can bite, but he is not known to."

Puppies begin their lives as mouthers and nippers. It is part of their play and positioning (in the pack). Though the bite of a puppy may sound harmless, they can actually be quite painful, as their new teeth are unworn and very sharp. Your Great Dane's puppy teeth will be able to pierce most types of clothing and other materials. This is why puppy chewing is often so damaging.

Helpful Hints

Do Dogs Feel Pain?

Since dogs seem to tolerate injuries more than humans, some people come to the conclusion that dogs do not feel much pain. The truth is that dogs have the same number of pain receptors as humans do. However, survival instincts may keep your Great Dane from showing signs of pain, so as not to appear helpless. He may also know that resting is the best way to heal. So when a dog is crying or whimpering, it is often a sign of great pain and should be taken to the veterinarian. Similarly, a dog that becomes inactive or lethargic may need medical attention.

When your puppy starts biting you, it is a habit that needs to be stopped immediately. After all, as discomforting as a puppy bite might be, a bite from a full-grown Great Dane can be quite devastating. One way to break his biting habit is to react loudly and as if you were in pain. A sudden "ouch" or "yipe" will often cause him to stop biting. Because he is just playing, he will not want to hurt you. Puppies try to stop their littermates' biting the same way. Sometimes this will cause their littermates to stop playing—something you could try. In the off chance that this does not work, sometimes grasping and holding his tongue outside of his mouth for a moment in your hand can discourage mouthing, as he will find the tongue hold quite unpleasant.

A Great Dane that bites can cause serious injury, make you open to a lawsuit, and place him at risk for euthanasia. Such behavior is not to be ignored or accepted. Socialization can help curb this, but an aggressive dog is not something for a novice to deal with. Consult a veterinary behaviorist if your Great Dane shows signs of aggression toward people.

His tongue When a Great Dane licks you with his full tongue, you will know you've been licked! Licking is another basic canine behavior. It can be a form of communication and bonding tool with other canines. It is a way to keep clean or tend wounds. It can be a way to obtain food (by licking an adult's mouth a puppy may trigger a regurgitated meal). Domesticated dogs continue this tradition by licking the muzzles of dominant dogs. Your dog may also lick you as a sign that you are the leader or in hopes of getting a meal.

The Tail of a Great Dane

When people ask if your Great Dane bites, you might indicate that the other end is more dangerous. His tail can be the source of trouble in and out of the house. Inside, his quickly wagging tail can knock a 5-pound object off a table! Items like dishes, cups, vases, phones, and such can be easily swung to the ground and damaged.

His sturdy wag can also cause pain when whipped onto a body. Bruising is not unusual at the source of contact. It can also knock down smaller individuals such as children and pets.

His Criminal Side

He may become a bit of a thief around the house. And though he may steal, like Robin Hood he simply takes from those who have, to give to those who have not—which is himself. The height of a Great Dane

BE PREPARED! Restraining Your Dane's Tail

Great Danes have powerful tails. A very happy Great Dane may have a very active tail that could break open and bleed (aka "happy tail") or cause injury. With such a Great Dane, one may want to train him to settle his tail with a "no wag" or "tail" command. If this doesn't suffice, you could also have him wear a tail-restraint belt fashioned out of veterinary wrap and sports tape.

How to make a simple and easy tail belt

- Cut a 3–4 foot-long section of veterinary wrap.
- Loop the wrap around your Great Dane's waist and squeeze ends of veterinary wrap together (it will adhere to itself). Make sure it is not too tight—you should be able to fit your hand between the wrap and the dog.
- Cut a 5-inch section of sports tape.
- Tuck your Great Dane's tail between his hind legs so it is below the veterinary wrap.
- Take the sports tape, sticky side up, and let the tucked tail rest in the middle of the tape. The tip of the tail should be around 2–3 inches past the edge of the tape.
- Gently close the tape around the tail—but DO NOT seal the ends. Tape should be secure but NOT tight around the tail.
- Then take the ends of the tape and loop them through the veterinary wrap, pressing the tape ends together and sealing them.

Because of the low attachment of the tail to the restraint belt, your Great Dane should be able to urinate and defecate if need be while wearing it.

makes it quite easy for him to get items off of countertops, desks, and tables. It is important that as a puppy, he be taught the manners to "leave" items alone that are not meant for him. He should never feel that taking food from a plate or table is acceptable or "cute," as many foods can be unhealthful or even poisonous for him, not to mention potentially making you go without.

Fear

No matter how large a dog is, he can have fears, even irrational ones. Common fears are fears of the new and unfamiliar whether they are locations, people, dogs, noises, falling objects, or something else. Although many Great Danes are outgoing, some individuals are more sensitive and just need a little more time to adjust to new things.

If your Great Dane has fears, the best approach is to gradually reintroduce the feared object or situation. Let him explore the situation. Use your body language to help him relax. If he sees you are not worried, it will have a calming effect. Often, laughing at the feared object will help him relax. In contrast, your getting upset or tense at his fears will only heighten his stress level. And never try to force him to confront a fearful situation. This will only be negative and simply increase his fear.

Another approach to calming a dog's fear is using another pet as a mentor. It can become a case of monkey see, monkey do. When the Great Dane sees another family member (a fellow canine would be best) not worried about an object or situation, he will more than likely follow the lead of the other pack member and relax.

Finally, never coddle your Great Dane when he is frightened. Your first response may be to protect and mother him, but this will give him the impression that he is correct in feeling this subject should be feared and that such a reaction will get a positive response: more attention. Once ingrained, it will be difficult to eliminate.

Fear response is another problem that can often be avoided with proper socialization when young. Still, irrational fears are just that: irrational. Your Great Dane may develop a fear of almost anything, for any reason, at any time. Be aware of such fears and if possible treat them as soon as they are discovered.

Separation Anxiety

Separation anxiety is a natural behavior formed in puppyhood and part of the dog's natural desire to be part of the pack and close to his mother. Like a human child who suddenly finds himself lost in a store, a dog can feel abandoned when his people are not around. In small doses, this may be amusing to some. The idea that their Great Dane worries when they are gone seems an endearing trait and proof of love.

The truth is, separation anxiety is a serious emotional condition that can become not only annoying as the Great Dane grows, but dangerous. A dog

suffering from separation anxiety can exhibit his fears in varying ways. Barking, drooling, whining, pacing, and panting are some of the more common signs. Dangerous and destructive activities include digging, chewing, and attempts at escape.

Getting your Great Dane over his separation anxiety will not be easy. The most common treatment is to not create cues about your plans. When he knows you are leaving, he starts to fret. Don't say the same thing or turn on the radio every time you leave. These can actually be warning signals about your imminent departure. Be aware of the types of visual cues he may notice like putting on shoes, picking up a purse, taking a coat, or such. One thing that can help is to make these things less certain. Randomly pick up your keys or grab a coat and after a few moments put them back. This will make him less sensitive to these actions.

Try developing a verbal cue for short trips, like "We'll be back soon." Start by saying it and leaving for just a few moments, and then return. Gradually lengthen the moments. This will let him know there are times you will be back soon. And use it only when the trip is brief. Sometimes increasing exercise may help, as it can tire him out. Anxiety takes a lot of energy, and a bored dog is more likely to be full of anxiety.

Despite these attempts, some Great Danes are extremely sensitive and people oriented. They may continue to experience separation anxiety no matter what you try. There are a variety of antianxiety drugs on the market. Most are canine versions of human prescriptions. There is debate in the medical community at how effective they are with anxiety. (A number of tests show they are more helpful in aggression than anxiety.) Some studies indicate the drugs can worsen the condition.

Breed Needs

Great Danes are one of the breeds highly susceptible to separation anxiety. Although some find such devotion endearing, and even appealing, it is an issue to be aware of and prepared for, as it could escalate to physical problems in some Great Danes. The best time to deal with this issue is when the dog is young.

Recently, dogs returning from overseas military duty have been increasingly diagnosed with anxiety disorders. This has created renewed interest in treatment—medically and psychologically. Perhaps as more research is done, the future will hold some solutions.

Behavior Problems and Solutions

Canines may be divine, but even the best can have problems. Bad habits are simply that, habits. Many behavior problems can be prevented in puppyhood. Should these habits be allowed to mature with the dog, they become more of a problem, but they are still correctable. In giant breeds, like Great Danes, behavior problems are magnified. Unfortunately, shelters and rescues are full of dogs that became "too difficult" to handle. Many of these problems could have been corrected if the owners had taken the time to deal with them.

Chewing An adult Great Dane has a very large and powerful (did we mention large?) mouth and thus the ability to chew on and through almost anything. When he is a puppy, you will need to direct his mouth toward appropriate objects (toys, chewies, bones, hard snacks) and away from personal items such as shoes, socks, furniture, or fingers.

Digging Being larger than many breeds, Great Danes can dig craters as if trying to unearth dinosaurs. One common method to discourage digging is to bury some of his own feces (excrement) into the hole he dug. Usually this makes him uninterested in continuing at that spot.

Scavenging Because of the dangers of some food items to a dog, it is important that you make certain that scavenging is not allowed. When you take him for a walk or outing, be aware of your surroundings for possible spills and dropped food. He may snap up a piece of garbage on the ground and gulp it down before you even have a chance to see what it was.

The Great Dane Senses

Just like humans, your Great Dane has five senses. However, he uses them somewhat differently than we do.

His Sense of Smell

A dog's sense of sense of smell is perhaps his most important. He uses it not just to distinguish things, but to analyze them. That is why when dogs meet, they spend a good deal of time sniffing each other's mouth, ears, genitalia, and anus. Your Great Dane will most likely try to similarly identify humans by sniffing their crotches and rears, which can be a bit embarrassing. Canines also get information from droppings and urine produced by other dogs.

His sense of smell is almost one thousand times stronger than your own. Whereas your olfactory sensors (the parts of your nose that can identify

FYI: The Smell of Fear

As the cliché goes, yes, a dog can smell fear. When humans have a fear or nervous reaction, they often sweat more, but not only the smell of their breath changes. A dog can detect the change in the human's body chemistry (this is why some dog show handlers may attempt to mask the smell of their nervous breath with gum or mints while in the ring). A dog will add this smell to other clues, including visual (posturing) and audio (vocal pitch change) to determine the human's fear, nervousness, or anxiety level.

smells) are about the size of a postage stamp, his are about the size of an 8.5-by-11 inch sheet of paper!

Humans have used this power for centuries. Hounds were used to aid in hunting by "sniffing out" prey. In the twentieth century the canine nose was put to use in locating lost people, and finding victims under rubble and snow. Law enforcement enlisted dogs to identify drugs and explosives. There is even evidence that some dogs can detect illnesses such as cancer and sense oncoming seizures.

His Sense of Hearing

As with his superior ability at smelling, your Great Dane can also hear a lot more than you. It is a well-known fact that dogs can hear higher pitches than humans, the reasons for those famed dog whistles. The range of sounds humans can hear is usually 20–20,000 Hertz (Hz—a measurement of audio based on cycles per second). Canines can also hear that range, but their top limit extends even higher. Pavlov, the scientist famous for showing that sound can create a physical reaction, was able to prove that a dog could hear 75,000 Hz.

Along with more pitch, he can hear things farther away than you. Hence he may react to noises you cannot hear, such as a distant bark or voice. And he can analyze the sound. Dogs can actually distinguish one car's engine noise from another, which is why your Great Dane knows you are home before you even get to the front door. With such keen hearing, you should never have to raise your voice. He can hear you. In fact, whisper a word he likes (*"Eat,"* *"Cookie," "Go bye-bye"*) and you will see how well he can hear you.

Do not be fooled if he seems oblivious to some noise. Even though you may hear a car door slam or the approach of a person to your home before he reacts, he could just be in such a relaxed state that he has tuned it out. If he doesn't respond to a command, he may simply be ignoring you. Remember, since he hears "more" than you do, and is analyzing what he hears, he may not always recognize what you think are the important commands. That is why you should speak his name when beginning to talk to him to get his attention.

His Sense of Vision

Whereas your Great Dane's ears and nose are far more sensitive than yours, when it comes to eyes, you have some advantage. However, he does not see "less" than you, he just sees things differently. Just ask anyone who uses dogs in hunting.

Your Great Dane does see color, despite the old belief. He just sees "less" color. His eye has fewer color receptors than yours. His receptors are more attuned to the blue-violet range and the green-yellow range, giving him a color sense similar to a human who is red-green colorblind. A blue-green light to you may appear as white or gray to him. Studies show that his eyes have a much stronger ability to differentiate subtle shades of gray. This not only helps him tell the difference in items of varied colors, but also aids in night vision.

Another way your Great Dane sees differently from you is in his peripheral vision. With his eyes set farther apart in his skull than you, he can see a wider range. The average human has a peripheral vision of around 180 degrees; he may see up to 250 degrees! This means he may be more aware of things occurring, or approaching, around him than you are.

But when it comes to depth perception, the humans win again. Tests show that a human's perception is approximately 140 degrees of binocular vision. Your Great Dane's is more likely to be in the 30–60 degree range, less than half that of a person's. This is why some Great Danes may not be as adept in catching tossed treats or toys as others. Yet despite this lower range, it is obvious that he is using other clues, ranging from brightness to shadows to aerial perspective. That is why in everything from hunting to playing fetch, your Great Dane can go the distance; he just sees it differently.

His Sense of Taste

Though some believe a dog's scavenger nature will cause him to eat anything, everyone who has ever lived with any dog knows he can be as finicky about his eats as a food critic or connoisseur. The taste buds in your mouth may be more sensitive than his, but since taste

Breed Truths

20-20 Vision?

Most tests show that the average canine has a vision of around 20/75. This means that a dog must be 20 feet from an object to clearly visualize details that a human with normal vision could clearly visualize from a distance of 75 feet. But for the dog in the wild, there is little need for such distinction of detail compared with its need to see movement and have improved night vision.

and scent are closely related, his powerful sense of smell probably levels the playing field. Something we have in common with our canine companions is the ability to associate illness with specific foods. For example, a dog that gets sick after eating a particular item may resist that food in the future. Tests have shown that most eating preferences are set as puppies. It has been found that many dogs prefer the foods they were fed as puppies and may resist newer diets (just like many people).

His Sense of Touch

Touch is the first sense nurtured as a puppy. Without official hands to touch, dogs use their whole body for touching. Dogs walking together will bump into each other frequently. This is considered a canine "handshake" or back pat. Great Danes will lean on people to show affection. They will rest a head on your lap. They will lie up against you in bed. It is all about touching and being touched.

The act of touch has been proven to be therapeutic for both you and your Great Dane. More and more medical evidence shows that petting your dog is good for you. It can reduce blood pressure as well as stress. Similarly a touching technique first developed on horses can aid your Great Dane. Called T-Touch, it is a form of specific touches and massage created by Linda Tellington-Jones. This process stimulates the mental and physical connections of your dog.

Just remember that canines and humans may enjoy different types of contact. Your Great Dane may prefer rubbing to hugging. The head, chest, and back are where many canines will enjoy getting the most physical attention. Touch itself can also be a positive reward for proper behavior.

The Local Climate

Great Danes can be affected by the weather and its changes as much as their human owners. In colder climates, Great Danes may need special protection. Their coats are short and they have a great deal of skin surface that can lose warmth. Although your dog may or may not enjoy being out in cold weather or snow, any extended activity outside should include wearing a coat. Since most commercial dog coats are too small for Great Danes, a foal or miniature-horse blanket are ideal. Feet can be cut by snow refrozen into ice crystals. Also be aware of chemical dangers in the winter, including salt used to melt ice and antifreeze drippings.

When the sun rules the skies, remember he can get overheated too. If the climate gets particularly hot, you will want to keep activity levels low in midday. Make sure he has plenty of water to drink and shaded/covered areas to lie in. Children's wading pools are great cooling-off areas and double as giant water bowls. You may also wish to consider cooler coats and cooler collars—clothing that you wet before you put on him. Both can be found through various pet supply stores, or made at home, and help keep your dog cool. If he is out in the sun a lot, and is of light pigment (for example Harlequin or white) you may wish to get sunscreen for him.

SHOPPING LIST

Extreme Weather Needs

Great Danes can do well in all climates, but for comfort and health reasons, one should be prepared for extreme conditions.

✔ Coat for cold weather—These can be official dog coats, or coats for foals and miniature horses.

✔ Heavy blankets—When temperatures drop, Great Danes enjoy snuggling into thicker bedding. Just beware of blankets with batting. If the blanket rips, your dog may ingest it.

✔ Coat for warm weather—Though it seems like an oxymoron, cooler coats are great for keeping your Great Dane cool in the summer. These coats are made of an absorbent material that you wet before you put on your dog.

✔ Spray bottle—When the temperature gets into the 90s, a spray bottle of water to spritz on your Great Dane can be a true comfort. Spraying his belly and genital areas will give him maximum relief.

✔ Sunscreen—The areas of your Great Dane that are light in pigment (i.e., white or pink) can get sunburned. Some of the best kinds of sunscreen are waterproof ones made specifically for young children.

Chapter Six

Health and Nutrition

Caring for your Great Dane, and helping him to live a long and happy life, begins with monitoring his health and nutrition. Although some may focus on the medical needs for the breed's maintenance, it really starts with the building blocks of your Great Dane: genetics and nutrition. Genetics are something you are dealt. But nutrition is how you play the hand.

Genetics and a Dane

Just as the genetics of your Great Dane's parents contributed to his coloring, they also can have input into his health. That is why it is so important to find out as much as possible about your Great Dane's relations. For example, if his parents and ancestors had long, healthy lives, he may be graced with the same. Should there have been health problems, your pup could be genetically predisposed to the same situation. In other words, just because his father had a condition (such as dysplasia, cancer, or heart disease) it does not mean he will get the condition, but he may be more susceptible to developing it.

Great Danes that are considered purebred are ones that for multiple generations have been bred only to other Great Danes. Although this is beneficial in the ways of creating a breed so that these dogs may resemble the image of the ideal Great Dane, it also makes their gene pool limited. Because of this limitation, the chances of a puppy inheriting the same recessive genes that can cause health issues from both parents are increased. (A recessive gene is one that produces its characteristics only when there are two of them—one from each parent.) Health, however, isn't something that comes from genes alone; it can be affected by environmental factors as well as nutrition.

Feeding Your Great Dane

Great Dane owners have many feeding options available. There are more brands and formulas for pet food on the market today than ever before. When planning a food regimen for your Great Dane, the first thing to consider is what your dog really needs. The multiple news reports of pet food

FYI: Who's Your Daddy?

To get an idea of how recessive genes can affect a puppy, color that can easily be seen will be used as example. You see a litter of Great Dane puppies. Mom is a Mantle. Dad is a Harlequin. Yet there is a Fawn-colored Mantle pup in the litter. Is someone not telling you something? Did Mom have a fling with a Fawn? No. Believe it or not, this coloring can and does happen. The Fawn colored puppy inherited one recessive Fawn gene from Mom and one from Dad.

Basically, there are two types of genes—recessive and dominant. Think of it as weak and strong genes. The dominant, "strong" genes can affect a puppy all by themselves. So one dominant gene from either parent can affect the puppy. But a recessive, "weak" gene needs help. It can affect the puppy only if it gets two—one from each parent.

Even the grandparents may not be Fawn. Being recessive, the gene could be 20 generations back or more until the Fawn is discovered. It is only when both parents have a recessive gene that it can come forward in a puppy.

Also of note is that even though it is one of the more common colors, Fawn is a recessive color. So is Blue. The most dominant color gene in Great Danes is Black. More about Great Dane colors on page 154.

recalls have made today's pet owners more conscious of the ingredients in their pets' foods.

Great Danes, like all dogs, are omnivores with a big emphasis on the carnivore side. They thrive on meat-based nutrition. Many commercial dog foods have grains listed in their ingredients. Because dogs do not fully process and use these grains, the owner must deal with them in the (literal) end in the large amount of waste that is produced. Also, the soluble part of the grain ferments in the intestines, creating gas, just as it does in humans. Today, there are a growing number of commercial pet foods that are "grain-free."

When shopping, look at the ingredients label. You can also see the ingredients of many commercial dog foods at *www.dogfoodanalysis.com*. And don't let your dog's "tastes" or finicky nature drive your decisions. Remember, if he is used to a low-quality diet, he may resist more healthful foods—just as a child may prefer candy and fast food over fruits and vegetables.

Commercial Dog Foods

The pet food industry, around since World War I, has exploded over the past few decades. It was once a fairly easy choice: canned or dry. Now, commercial dog food takes up a whole aisle in many stores. There are foods advertised for every size and age of dog. There are those that promise more meat or more vegetables. Some aim at the economical shopper, others at the pampered pooch. Yet, as with any processed foods, you should pay attention to what you are putting into your Great Dane.

To simplify the discussion, we will split commercial dog foods into three types: the standard, the limited grain, and the no (or little) grain. To tell which are which, check the ingredients list. Ingredients are listed based on highest percentages first, so percentage-wise, there is more of the first item listed. Those that offer lots of meat at the beginning are generally better than those that start off with grain. Be aware that many companies list an ingredient several ways to lower the apparent percentage. For example, some list corn, cornmeal, and corn flour as three separate ingredients. That keeps "corn" from being one of the first ingredients even though it should be.

Many standard brands have been around for years, and are generally lower

Breed Needs

Feeding High or Low

There is much debate on whether Great Danes should be fed from an elevated bowl or not. Information on this subject alone is very contradictory. Some suggest that feeding from an elevated rise means less air is swallowed. They argue this aids in reducing the risk of bloat. However, studies at Purdue University concluded that dogs fed from elevated bowls had a higher chance of developing bloat.

in cost. Though they may not be the most healthful food, many generations of dogs have lived on them. These foods often have a majority of by-products and grain (usually corn or wheat) in their ingredients. Be aware that by-products ("beef by-products," etc.) can be any part of the cow. However, you should avoid any food that has mystery meat—listed as "meat by-products."

Helpful Hints

Grains and Danes

There is a great deal of discussion these days about the problems of grain in commercial dog foods. Some feel grains should be totally eliminated. The truth is that human-grade whole grain in moderation can add valuable carbohydrates. Many commercial foods use processed grains, which do not have sufficient nutrient value. And many use it as the main ingredient. Over the years, a number of food recalls have been caused by contaminated grain.

There is no way to know what kind or kinds of animal meats might have been used.

Limited-grain foods are frequently sold as more healthful choices. They often use rice and potato as a binder instead of wheat and corn. (Some suggest that the rising price of corn may be a factor in this decision.) Many of these entries do not use any meat by-products, instead opting for real meat. Prices can vary depending on brand, but they are usually higher than the heavy-grain brands. Again, it's always smart to look at the labels to see what is really included.

Grain-free brands are relatively new on the scene. They are an attempt by the major manufacturers to tap into a growing market of those looking for more healthful food. These foods should not be confused with a raw diet (see below). All of the meat has been processed and many nutrients have been cooked out. Also, they may not be totally grain-free, but they can be a practical alternative to feeding a raw diet. Because of the higher protein percentage of calories, grain-free brands are not recommended for young puppies.

Canned Versus Dry

Some may think that canned foods are simply dry food with water added. Although that may almost be the case with some brands, it is not a universal truism. Basically, canned foods are not ideal as the entire diet for a Great Dane, but can be given as a tasty treat or even for hiding medication. Canned food, being soft, has a tendency to stick to the teeth and can create problems with gums and teeth. Dry food, although better for the teeth, may be soaked with water before a feeding. Some believe that the swelling of dry food in the belly can be a precursor to bloat. (A study by Purdue University noted a link between soaking dry food before eating and cases of bloat.) If you feed kibble, you may wish to do a soak test to see how much the brand swells. Some kibble can be sponge-like, expanding two to three times its dry size. Such swelling would be better done outside the body than in.

Fun Facts

Some view raw diets as a fad. Actually, meats, organs, and bones (often served with leftovers) have been standard pet nutrition for centuries. It is pet food that is the fad, having been created around World War I. The first commercial dog food was canned horse meat (allegedly for the purpose of making profit off of dead horses). By the 1930s dry chows and cat food were added. After World War II it became a major business. So the idea of prepared pet foods (a source of income from previously discarded meat and grain by-products) isn't even a century old.

Feeding What Comes Naturally

The Great Dane is a canine. His ancestor is the wolf, a canine that hunted for food. He ate a diet of raw meat, bones, and organs from the animals his pack brought down. His diet rarely included grains, unless it was in the belly of his recent catch.

Today that tradition lives on with those who choose to feed raw diets, which are sometimes referred to as B.A.R.F—biologically appropriate raw food or a prey model diet. A raw diet focuses on giving your dog the nutrition he needs, in a form that is also beneficial to his all-around health. For example, the lack of grains will shorten digestion time, and reduce stool size and gas as well. The bones and extensive chewing can aid in keeping your Great Dane's teeth clean of tartar accumulation.

To many, the idea of giving a dog chicken with bones is unhealthful because of the constant stories about choking on chicken bones. The difference is that a raw bone is flexible and digestible. It is when cooked that bones dry out and can splinter, increasing the possibility of injuring a dog.

Most zoos feed their own canine charges a form of raw diet. Some veterinarians are quick to point out that domesticated dogs have come a long way from the wolf. But as more research becomes available, veterinarians are beginning to consider the benefits of a well-balanced approach to a raw diet. Dr. Ian Billinghurst, an Australian Veterinarian, began researching and developing a healthful diet for canines. His first book, *Give Your Dog a Bone*, was

FYI: Satin Balls Recipe

If you need to add a bit of weight to your Great Dane, Satin Balls are a tasty and healthful way to do so. There are a variety of recipes available, and as any chef will tell you, a little experimenting can lead to exciting discoveries. But below are the standard ingredients many use.

  10 pounds raw hamburger meat
  10 eggs
  1 cup vegetable oil
  1 jar wheat germ
  8 cups uncooked oatmeal
  1 cup unflavored molasses
  2 pounds Total cereal (a large box) *
  10 packs unflavored gelatin

Mix the ingredients in a large bowl. Roll into balls. Refrigerate (or freeze) and serve.

Variations include adding garlic or salt for flavor. Satin Balls are fed raw.

*Total cereal is used because it has a multivitamin already added.

published in 1993. Since then he has become a leader in the cause to bring positive nutrition via a raw diet.

To gain the benefits of a raw diet, one does not need to become a butcher, cutting up raw meat, organs, and bones. Feeding raw to your Great Dane can actually be as easy as pouring kibble or plopping canned dog food into his bowl, as there are many packaged raw products readily available today.

Overweight Greats

Great Danes are a giant breed. But that means giant in height, not weight. When they carry extra weight, it is hard on their backs, joints, hearts, and other organs. (A recent study showed that dogs eating 25 percent less food lived an average of 15 percent longer.) Gauge how much to feed your Great Dane by how much he eats and how much he weighs. In a growing Great Dane, it is important to keep him lean. A waist should be visible from the side at any age. You should be able to see the hint of the last two ribs before his waistline. With a mature adult, you should be able to feel (but not see) the ribs slightly when you run your hands along the rib cage.

A potbellied Great Dane could be a sign of internal parasites or other serious illness. Most rounded or sausage-looking Great Danes are fat because they are fed too much. For their health they need to lose weight. For the Great Dane who acts like he is always starving, you can help appease him and keep the calorie count lower by adding a can of green beans to his food.

Over-the-counter diet foods are often not much lower in calories than standard food, so do not expect a lot from them. Also take care to not feed too many snacks. They can really cause the calorie count to skyrocket.

It is not uncommon for Great Danes to be thin while growing. But thinness in an adult may be indicative of a problem. It could be illness, a digestive disorder, possibly too much activity or anxiety, or simply not enough food. If the possibility of health problems has been eliminated, try adding Satin Balls, or higher-calorie dog food rolls, or some ground beef. You can even add an extra meal or give some treats in the evening before bed.

Choosing a Veterinarian

No matter the genetic nature of your Great Dane, or how well you feed him, like all of us, eventually he'll need medical attention. If possible, locate a veterinarian that you feel comfortable with before you need one.

A good veterinarian is the combination of several factors.

Helpful Hints

To Be Sure, Insure

Just as you buy insurance for yourself, health insurance for your pet is available. As with human insurance, there are various plans. Some cover everything anywhere; others cover limited visits, procedures, even specific veterinarians or hospitals. Be sure to read all the details, and ask your veterinarian if there are plans they already work with. These plans can save you money and could be a wise investment. However, if you have multiple dogs, it could be costly to buy coverage for each of them.

- **Location.** You want to be certain medical help is nearby in case of an emergency. If your veterinarian's hospital does not have 24-hour availability, it is important to locate a second facility that does.
- **Experience.** It's a good idea to seek a veterinarian who has experience with giant breeds. Not only may that person be more equipped to handle the size of your Great Dane but he or she will often have more knowledge about what he may need.
- **Bedside Manner.** It is always better for you and your Great Dane to find a doctor you can easily talk to. Since your Great Dane cannot talk to you, you will want a veterinarian who can explain to you what may be happening and what needs to be done to help.

Visiting the Veterinarian

There are a number of reasons to visit your veterinarian, beyond an illness or an emergency. The most important may be an annual checkup. After all, each year of your dog's life equals around four to seven human years. That is more than enough time for his health to change. These annual visits will usually include a visual check. Blood may be drawn, and depending on what initial signs point to, fecal or urine samples may be requested.

Like a visit to your doctor when you are sick, your veterinarian will base a good deal of his actions on what you tell him. This is when you describe any symptoms or oddities you have noticed about your Great Dane. Here are some signs that should alert you that your Great Dane may not be feeling well:

- vomiting
- coughing
- loss or increase of appetite
- weakness, lethargic behavior
- open sores
- sleeping more or less than usual
- change in urination or bowel habits and consistencies
- swelling of abdomen or chest
- trembling
- temperature change
- blood in stool or urine
- any real change in your Great Dane's regular routine/behavior

Based on your information and the preliminary exam, the veterinarian may request any variety of tests from X-rays to ultrasounds. Depending on his or her diagnosis, a trip to a specialist may be recommended.

Doing a Home Checkup

At any sign of injury or illness, it is wise to err on the side of safety. There are many things you can check at home to better diagnose any problem. This information will also help when you see the veterinarian. After all, the veterinarian will be spending only minutes with your Great Dane, whereas you have spent your life with him.

Gum Color

The color of a healthy Great Dane's gums is often a deep pink, though in a dark-pigmented dog they may be brownish in color. You can check his capillary refill by pressing a thumb to his gum a moment and then removing it. His gum color should return to pink (or their normal color) within a few seconds. If it takes longer, he may be having circulation problems. Pale gums can be a sign of anemia or blood loss. Bluish gums can indicate a lack of oxygen or poor circulation. Red could be a sign of fever, overheating, intestinal blockage, or toxicity.

Lethargic Behavior

A lethargic Great Dane could be suffering from any number of ailments. It could be an infection, anemia, general pain, or stomach issues.

Breed Truths

Longevity

Great Danes are not long lived among dog breeds. You can expect a healthy Great Dane to live an average of 7–10 years. Some may be blessed to live into their double digits.

Temperature

Just as in humans, an unusual temperature (lower or higher than normal) can indicate an illness or injury. Luckily, it is not difficult to take a Great Dane's temperature because of his size. If taking a puppy's rectal temperature you may need to lubricate the thermometer for his comfort. However, an adult Great Dane may not need any lubricant at all. Although in this day and age there are thermometers that can take a reading aurally (from the ear,) the tried-and-true rectal style is best. The average temperature for a dog is 101–102°F (38.3–38.9°C).

If it rises above 104°F, you should get your Great Dane to the veterinarian. Should it rise above 105°F, immediately try cooling him down with wet towels on his body or rubbing alcohol on his paws (this causes evaporation, which will help to cool him) while on your way to the animal hospital. Should it drop below 98°F, he also needs to see a veterinarian. Should it fall

FYI: Pilling Your Great Dane

Some Great Danes may be able to take their medication by the "hide-it" method. That is where you cover a pill by sticking it in a slice of cheese, a piece of hot dog, or some meat. There are even treats that are hollow, such as Pill Pockets, for this purpose. If your dog will not take the pills "hidden," you will need to give them to him manually. Luckily, an adult Great Dane has a large enough head (and mouth) to make pilling not too difficult—unless he refuses. Here is one way to pill your dog:

- Facing your Great Dane place your hand on his muzzle and tilt his head back.
- Gently fold his upper lip with your thumb over his teeth as you open the mouth. This may help make him keep his mouth open so he doesn't accidentally bite his own lip.
- Raise your thumb to the roof of your Great Dane's mouth. Hold the pill in your other hand between your thumb, index, and middle fingers.
- Push the pill back over his tongue to his throat and release the pill. (It is possible to push the pill somewhat down the throat at this time.) Then immediately close the mouth and blow on the dog's nose, which will encourage him to swallow. Stroking the throat may also aid in getting your Great Dane to swallow. If you are unable to get the pill far enough back, he may spit it out.

The first time you try, it may be difficult. But with practice, you should find it fairly easy, as adult Great Danes typically have a spacious mouth.

below 97°F, begin warming him with blankets. A newborn or very young Great Dane puppy can be put under your shirt.

Pulse

A high or low pulse rate can be a sign of illness and could indicate that a trip to the veterinarian is needed. To take your Great Dane's pulse, follow these easy steps.

- Have your Great Dane lie completely on his side.
- Place your hand under the top hind leg. (Your hand is now between his legs.)
- Find the crease that divides the lower leg from the body (groin).
- Put your index and middle fingers alongside the crease, which is where a main artery is located.
- Count the pulse beats for a full minute. If you have difficulty, you can count for 15 seconds and multiply by four.

A large dog's pulse is usually around 60 to 80 beats per minute. (The larger the dog, the slower the pulse should be.) Take the pulse two to three times during an hour, as the first time your Great Dane may get excited or nervous because of your handling of him. If the pulse of your dog deviates greatly from 60 to 80, you should take him to a veterinarian.

Diarrhea

One of the most common ailments in all dogs is diarrhea. The causes can be anything from diet to allergies to parasites to illness. If loose bowels are a single occurrence, there is no need for worry. Even seeing a small amount of blood in the stool may not be of immediate concern. Bright red blood indicates bleeding near the anus, whereas dark red blood usually means bleeding in the higher digestive tract. Continued diarrhea, or diarrhea along with vomiting, fever, and pain, indicates a serious problem that you should notify your veterinarian about.

At the first sign of diarrhea it may be wise to withhold food for around 24 hours to see if that clears it up. After that time, feed easily digestible selections like boiled chicken. Young puppies (under six months of age) should not fast; if possible simply feed small, low-fat meals. If diarrhea persists, take a stool sample to your veterinarian and have it tested for parasites and illness. If the tests come up negative, ask your veterinarian about using anti-diarrhea treatments. One natural aid is to feed a small amount of canned pumpkin. (Make sure it does not have spices in it.) The natural fiber in pumpkin may help soothe and firm up stool. Your veterinarian may prescribe a medication or a probiotic food additive such as Fortiflora.

Health Concerns

As with many giant breeds, your Great Dane may begin to develop health issues with age. Most common among these are hip problems, bloat, bone cancer, and heart disease. Many of these issues can be agitated by excessive weight, so it is always a good idea to keep your dog lean.

Bloat

As Great Danes are a large, deep-chested breed, they are very susceptible to gastric dilatation (buildup of gas) and volvulus or gastric torsion (twisting), aka GDV, commonly referred to as the dreaded "bloat."

Bloat is a serious condition that can often turn fatal quickly wherein an abnormal amount of foam, fluid, or air accumulates within the stomach, causing it to swell. The affected dog is in a great deal of discomfort and may attempt to retch to relieve the pressure.

However, he may not be able to, as his stomach can actually twist between the esophagus and upper intestines, trapping this buildup inside and cutting off vital blood flow. This can put him at risk of cardiac problems and shock, not to mention causing his organs to die and toxic buildup to be produced. Bloat can occur with or without twisting.

A study conducted by Purdue University School of Veterinary Medicine in 1998 reported that Great Danes as a breed are 40 times more likely to develop GDV (bloat) than a dog of mixed breeding. The study also said that assuming these Great Danes live to be 10 years of age, "we conservatively estimate that more than 50 percent will eventually suffer an episode of GDV." In their study, Great Danes were at the top of the vulnerable breeds list, with the highest incident of GDV—which was nearly twice the risk to the second breed on the list, the Akita.

Symptoms of bloat may include the following:

- heavy panting
- drooling
- gagging (as if to vomit)
- an extended or hard abdomen (often resembling a basketball)
- vomiting very frothy foam
- pacing
- abnormal stretching
- odd-colored gums (red, blue, or white)
- whining
- anxiety
- weakness and collapsing.

Bloat is a life-threatening emergency and your Great Dane may have only 30 minutes after symptoms have been identified, so if you suspect your Great Dane is experiencing a bloat episode, get him to the veterinarian ASAP! You must not "wait and see" if he improves. You also cannot wait for your veterinarian to open. This is a time when knowing the location of a 24-hour emergency center is essential.

In bloat cases where torsion has occurred, surgery is required. The veterinarian may recommend a gastropexy, where the dog's stomach is actually stapled or sutured to the inside of his body, often to his rib cage. Although it may not prevent future bloat incidents, it will lessen the chance that the stomach itself will twist. An incident of bloat can be very expensive, running into thousands of dollars, especially if emergency rooms are needed.

Talk with your veterinarian about preventive measures for bloat. Some veterinarians recommend a prophylactic gastropexy surgery. Some may even be able to perform a less invasive technique in which the stomach is tacked laparoscopically. A scope is inserted into the stomach through the throat and a slight incision is made to attach the stomach to the side. This procedure can be done as early as six months of age.

In regard to bloat, the Purdue University study suggested that diet was a key factor. Factors the study found that increased the chance of bloat in dogs included the following:

- feeding only once a day
- feeding very large meals
- feeding a dry food with fat as one of the first ingredients
- soaking dry food in water

Other factors found in the study included speed of eating (dogs that wolfed or gobbled their food were more susceptible), age (chances for bloat increase almost 20 percent for every year the dog ages), and family history. Two long-believed theories—that exercise and/or drinking around mealtime increased the risk of bloat—were found to have no association.

Ask your veterinarian how you may be better prepared for bloat, and what you may be able to do for your Great Dane should it occur. Things to inquire about include simethicone (available in pills and liquid form) and how to pass a stomach tube. Emergency bloat kits can be purchased from Nature's Farmacy (*www.NaturesFarmacy.com*).

Once a Great Dane has bloated, he is at a higher risk to bloat again. So even if your dog did not require surgery, you may wish to speak with your veterinarian about preventive procedures.

Bone Cancer

Canine bone cancer (osteosarcoma) is one of the most common types of cancer in dogs, often showing up on the leg. The cancer starts on the surface of the bone and progresses to the center. Symptoms of bone cancer can develop over a short period of time or may show as persistent lameness that doesn't respond to sprain or joint injury remedies. The treatment of choice is to

CAUTION

Full Moons

The moon is known to move the tides of the ocean. Considering that bodies are about 70 percent water, it is no wonder that some believe Great Danes can also be affected by the moon.

It is not uncommon for sensitive dogs to have a belly upset around the week of a full moon. If your Great Dane appears to be affected during this time with symptoms such as air licking, excessive gas, and an overwhelming desire to eat lots of grass, you may be able to help reduce the chance of bloat by giving him a few simethicone gel caps with each meal during the week of the full moon.

One possible reason for some Great Danes to be affected around full moons may be internal parasites. Scientists have found that parasites are most active and often reproduce around the full moon. Hence even a small number of parasites, which may not be detected, could disrupt your dog's internal tract during this time.

remove the tumor, frequently by limb amputation, but it is seldom successful for long. Bone cancer can also occur at other places, such as ribs or even the skull. Symptoms for these areas could include a hard lump (on a rib) or nasal discharge, difficulty chewing and swallowing, and facial swelling. This usually happens in middle age or older dogs. Sadly, in larger breeds, it can begin at a young age.

Heart Disease

Great Danes are particularly susceptible to dilated cardiomyopathy, also called DCM. This is where the heart muscle becomes weakened and stretched, so a chamber of the heart becomes enlarged. It causes the heart to pump inefficiently and causes fluid buildup in other areas of the body. Symptoms of heart disease may include fatigue, lethargy, and unwillingness to exercise, fainting, increased panting, a dry cough (particularly in the night and early morning), loss of appetite, and weight loss. Some dogs may develop a potbellied look and a gray tinge to their gums. The development of heart DCM is mostly associated with genetic factors; however, poor diet and obesity may accelerate it. DCM is often discovered in its final stages, and medication can comfort the patient, but once it is detected, the prognosis is not good.

Canine Hip Dysplasia (CHD)

Any dog can be afflicted with this disorder, but because of size and weight, larger breeds can be at higher risk. Symptoms of CHD include pain and discomfort during exercise, change in the dog's gait (such as running with the back legs doing a bunny hop), and stiffness. CHD is caused by a looseness of the hip joint creating abnormal wear of the joint and ultimately arthritis and pain. X rays will diagnose the condition, but CHD may not appear in a dog for years. CHD can be treated, but such treatments are costly. There are four surgical treatments usually recommended. 1) A total hip replacement is where the existing joint is removed and an artificial joint or prosthesis is implanted. 2) Femoral head and neck excision is where the head of the

femur (the ball that goes into the hip) is removed and a fibrous pseudo-joint replaces the hip. 3) In puppies under one year, a triple pelvic osteotomy can be performed. If there is lots of hip looseness, but no damage to the joints, the pelvic bones are broken and realigned to restore normal function. 4) Also available for pups under 20 weeks is juvenile pubic symphysiodesis, where the pelvic bones are fused together to allow the other bones to develop normally. Considered to be hereditary, CHD can appear even if no signs have been detected in the genealogy of the dog.

Megaesophagus

This is a condition where the tube that carries food, liquid, and saliva to the dog's stomach (the esophagus) fails to push things into the stomach. This is caused by a weakening of the muscles and enlargement of the esophagus. Symptoms include frequent regurgitation after eating, failure to thrive, and a high risk of chronic pneumonia caused by breathing in the liquids or solids. Megaesophagus can be congenital (wherein the puppy is born with it) or develop later in life. Once diagnosed, there is no treatment, only management through diet and positioning of the dog so gravity can pull the food down.

By being aware of genetics, nutrition and medicine, your Great Dane should be able to live a healthy, happy life with you. The key is to remember that you are the guardian angel for your Great Dane. Watch over him as he watches over you.

Chapter Seven

Training and Activities

U nlike small breeds, which can often function in crowds without major training, giant breeds must be well mannered. Their sheer size can create unintentional calamities. But with a few basics under your belt and their collar, Great Danes can make almost any outing more enjoyable for everyone.

Training Tools

The Command or "Cue" Word

Before you start the training process, you will need to settle on some "command" or "cue" words. These are the words you will use to tell your dog what you want. Choose one command word per task and stick to it. Everyone in the family should use the same word. Using multiple words for the same request may cause confusion. Be aware of words that you might use commonly that will trigger him when you don't want his response. Also remember that he may not be able to discern between similar-sounding words like *flip*, *slip*, and *clip*. If there is a task you do not want others to trigger, such as *speak* (barking), choose a word that is not easily guessed. Just don't make the commands difficult to remember, or so unique that others needing to work with your Great Dane (trainers, friends, etc.) will have difficulty controlling them.

Using a Clicker

A great tool for training your Great Dane is a clicker. Inexpensive to purchase and easy to use, it can become the perfect connection between your request and his response. A clicker can be used in a variety of fashions for training.

Basically, a clicker conditions a dog to know a reward is coming, much like Pavlov conditioned dogs to drool from the sound of a bell. An example of using a clicker would be telling your Great Dane to sit. As soon as his rump touches the ground, you click the clicker and then give a food reward. The sound of the clicker will eventually become the praise he will look forward to.

Since a click is not a word that he might hear, the clicker is a precise tool for training. For more information, check out *www.clickertraining.com*.

SHOPPING LIST

Training Gear

When you are ready to start training your new friend, you will need a few items.

✔ Collar—Because suggested methods do not rely on force, you may not need a chain collar (choke chain) for training. A buckle collar should suffice. If more control is needed, you may want to look into a prong, or pinch, collar. See page 68.

✔ Leash—You will want a 6-foot leash. A leather leash is a good choice, as it is durable, pliable, and won't burn your hands should it be pulled through them. Chain leashes are not recommended, as they are difficult to get a good grip on and can damage your hand if pulled on quickly.

✔ Clicker—A clicker can be beneficial, as it can help create a bridge between trick, command, and reward. A clicker need not be a store-bought one. You can even click your tongue to the roof of your mouth, which keeps your hands free.

✔ Flashlight—For deaf Great Danes, a flashlight can operate as a clicker. The light becomes the bridge for tricks and behavior.

Rewards and Rank

When beginning to work with your Great Dane, you will need the two essential elements of command: rewards and rank.

Rewards, more than force or punishment, will help create a happy, well-mannered puppy open to continued training. A "reward" does not have to be a treat. Training your dog with just treats can unintentionally teach him to respond only to food. This can cause you to become a walking treat bag, and him to become overweight. Praise should always be the reward given before any treat. Praise can be verbal or physical attention.

As you train your Great Dane, remember to praise him *every time* he does what you want. Once he seems to make the connection between the command and the act, begin to cut back on the treats. He should know that he will always get praise for doing the right thing.

Points to remember:

- Try to have several different kinds of treats on hand to add variety and surprise.
- Training should be done randomly so as not to create a "time" of when to behave.
- It is best to keep training time to short sessions and always end on a positive note.
- Be patient.

FYI: Consider a Group Training Class

Going to formal classes can be a way of finding the time to train your puppy. It can also aid in socializing. There are even puppy kindergarten classes. Check with your breeder about possible classes in your area. Your local kennel or obedience clubs may offer classes as well as some pet stores. You can check *www.akc.com* to help you find a local group and to look into the American Kennel Club's Star Puppy program.

Basic Commands

Come

The first command any dog should learn is *come*. Coming when called is essential behavior. When young, puppies will usually come to you for food or play. Anytime he comes to you, he should receive praise. The goal is to have him come to you when called.

This important training should start at an early age. A good way is for you to get your puppy's attention with verbal or physical sounds (clapping hands on your thighs, for example). Once your puppy notices the activity, he most likely will head toward you to investigate. At that point, say, "Apollo, come." When he arrives, praise him for coming to you. You can also use the *come* command when he comes for dinner to help enforce the term.

Here's a common way to teach *come* with older puppies:

CAUTION

Coming when called is not a game. He needs to come when you call and not run around playing keep-away. When situations get questionable, or even dangerous, he needs to come to you. It should also not be a threat. When you need your dog for something he may not like (such as a bath or medication), it is best to go to him. If he worries about coming to you, he will be reluctant to do so. Your Great Dane should never be afraid to come to you.

1. Place a collar on your Great Dane and clip a leash to the collar's ring. Walk a few steps away from him, keeping hold of the leash. Show him a toy or treat to attract his attention.
2. He should want to come to you. Once he begins to move to you, say *"Come"* to create association with the command and behavior. Praise him the moment he touches you. If desired, follow with a treat.
3. The goal is to be able to touch his collar or neck. If he comes near you, but stays out of reach, the command will be of little use.

As always, continue his training in new locations. If the area is not secure, a long lead—usually 10–30 feet—(3–9 m) can come in handy. Remember, most public places have laws that will require you to keep your dog on a leash at all times. For your Great Dane's safety be sure to respect these rules.

Heel

Any time you take your Great Dane out on a leash, he will need to know the *heel* command. The last thing you want is to be dragged down the street by him. As it is, you will hear plenty of "who's walking who" jokes when out in public. With a Great Dane (or other giant breed), a polite walk on-lead is not only pleasant, but can help prevent accidents.

When officially exhibiting a dog in conformation or any on-lead obedience, he is always walked on the left side. For that reason, it is best to train your dog to walk on your left.

1. Start with him standing or sitting on your left side. It is best to do this while he has a collar and leash attached. (Ideally he will in time be able to *heel* off-lead.)
2. Before you take a step, make sure he is paying attention, then say *"Heel"* and walk forward. If he comes to your side, praise him.
3. Repeat.

If he bounds ahead of you, turn around 180 degrees and walk in the opposite direction, repeating the *heel* command. If he pulls again, turn around 180 degrees again and step forward. If he loses focus and gets playful or excited, stand in place. Do not advance again until he is paying attention. In the beginning, some dogs may need treats to encourage a proper heel.

Stay

When living with a Great Dane, you will find the *stay* command a common request. The command is telling him to remain still in whatever position he currently is in. *Stay* can be done in a *stand*, *sit*, or *down* position. This will also be useful out in public. The command word is usually *"Stay"* or *"Hold"*.

> **Helpful Hints**
>
> As important as it is to have a command or cue word to start your Great Dane on a task, it is equally important to have a "release" word. This is the word that tells your Great Dane that the task, trick, or command is over—kind of an "at-ease" for your Great Dane. No matter how many command or cue words you may have, you should have only one release word. That word will tell your Great Dane it is no longer necessary to *stay*, *sit*, *lie*, etc.

1. Place him in a *sit* or *down* position. Stand in front of him and hold your hand to his face in a "stop" position. Follow this by saying, *"Stay."* After a few seconds, reward him and release him with a command word—("release" meaning that the task is over.)
2. Repeat the process, only now add a turn so that you are facing away from him. Wait a second or two and then turn back to face him. Always be sure to reward him before you give him the release word.
3. Once he is performing well, begin moving around after the command. Give the command and then step away, step to his side, and step behind him. The key is to have him remain still while you do another activity.
4. Finally, once you can move around him without issue, try adding a few distractions—other people, odd noises, toys, and such.

Once he is comfortable in the *stay* position, keep training in public areas. In such areas, keep him on a leash for safety. Your Great Dane should be able to be equally at ease in the *down-stay* and *stand-stay* positions. Be aware that he may "melt" into a *down* from a *sit-stay*. To strengthen his *sit-stays*, practice is the key.

Down

With a giant breed, having them lie down when you need them to is essential. When around other dogs and people, your dog's size could create nervousness. Having him lie down will make everyone more comfortable and should keep him out of harm's way. It is never too soon to begin teaching this command.

Breed Needs

Being a giant breed, Great Danes have large paws and very powerful legs. Be aware that some Great Danes may become overly enthusiastic with *shake* and may smack people with their large paw to get attention. Be sure your Great Dane knows that he should raise his paw at people only when requested.

1. Find a large enough location for you and him. He will need a lot of room when he is lying down.
2. Get him to sit (assuming he knows that command already). Using food or a toy, move it down and slowly forward, coaxing him to lower his body. As his elbows touch the ground, say "*Down!*" Reward with praise and a treat. If need be, guide him gently with pressure on his shoulders.
3. Repeat without treats, using only gestures and the command word.
4. Finally, begin the process from a standing position.

Stand

Another good command to teach is *stand*. This can be quite beneficial during veterinarian exams. It is also vital to know for conformation showing. *Stand* is trained much the same as the *stay*, but the Great Dane must remain on all four feet, and not go into a *sit* or *down*.

Leave It

Similar to *stay* or *stand*, *leave it* is a vital command for your Great Dane to know. The Great Dane's head height is frequently aligned with the tops of tables and counters. This makes it very easy for him to see, and sample things that he should not. *Leave it* can be easily taught.

Fun Facts

Dogs, like people, can be right or left handed (pawed). When doing tricks or activities that require your dog to hold up a paw, watch which one he frequently uses first. If he often signals with his right, he is most likely right pawed. If he primarily uses his left paw, he most likely is a lefty, or southpaw.

1. Place an item he would like (toy or treat) in a location he can reach (table, floor).
2. When he heads to it, simply tug if on a leash or make a harsh noise (like making the sound of a buzzer) followed by the words *Leave it* to indicate that the item is not to be touched.
3. Reward with praise.
4. Repeat with other items and locations.

This command is important when you are in public areas and prefer that he not reach for items (or even other pets) on the ground. The *leave it* command can prevent many unwanted ingestions and incidents.

Teaching Tricks

A Great Dane will usually attract a crowd of admirers because of his size when out in public. He may enjoy showing off a little, so giving him some special abilities will not only amuse onlookers, but give him a sense of fun. But tricks are just that: fun. They should never be confused with necessary commands like *come*, *stay*, and others.

High Five

It seems everyone expects a dog to "shake." With a little variation, this can be modified to something a bit showier. It can even be a "wave."

1. Stand in front of him and have him *sit*.
2. Raise your right hand toward his right paw (or your left to his left). If he does not lift his paw, you can take it in your hand. Reward him as soon as his paw is steady in your hand.
3. When he is lifting his paw in time to your hand, hold your hand flat, palm out.
4. Add the command *"High five."* Give him your hand and reward him when his paw connects with your hand and you are able to hold it.

Speak

Great Danes are not considered barkers, but they will bark at the usual times for alarm or play. While it may sound like a good idea to teach your Great Dane to speak/bark, be certain he understands when barking is desired and when it is not.

1. What causes your Great Dane to bark naturally? Is it outside noise? Television images? Sirens? Once you figure out what makes him bark, you can be prepared.

2. When you can tell his bark factor is about to happen, command him to *Speak* (or other word) before he does. Once he has barked, give praise and possibly a reward.
3. Try to spark a bark when no other factor is around. When he is successful, reward him.

Helpful Hints

Bilingual Canines

Some trainers will use a different language for commands to keep the public from using the commands for their dog such as "Speak."

When it comes to the command word, you may wish to use something other than *Speak*, since strangers and others may say it hoping for a reaction. Try something like *Woof* or maybe *Talk*. Just be certain it is not a word you use commonly so as not to have him *speak* at random. Also, remember that occasional barking is not a bad thing. Letting others know that this is his home is part of his character. Finally, as mentioned, many a Great Dane will not be prone to barking. Yours may tend toward the odd vocalizations from rumbling to slight whines. You can certainly try the above method to coax out some of his odder sounds.

Fun for All

All work and no play is no way to enjoy having a best friend. Your Great Dane may be part couch potato, but he will still want to get up and go. Once he has mastered basic commands and is controllable on a leash, you and he can explore the world and take part in a variety of activities. To prepare for your adventures outside, you will want to have a few items.

- A leash and collar that can handle at least 100 pounds
- Cleanup bags for droppings (with giant breeds you will need a good-size bag)
- A spare leash and collar, as even the best can break at an inopportune moment
- Water for drinking, cooling the coat/skin, and flushing out possible wounds

The easiest way to get out is to take walks around the neighborhood. Most local governments have leash laws, so please follow local guidelines. While walking neighborhood streets, be aware of your surroundings. Cars can come out of nowhere. Children can run up and startle. Unleashed dogs can approach. Pavement can get very hot. There are unknown foods on the ground that may make him sick.

If you live away from the city, where you can walk in fields, mountains, or the desert, there will be other challenges. There is the possibility of meeting wild animals that may have diseases. Depending on the area of the country you live in, you may need to worry about ticks and fleas. After walking through bushes, it is always recommended that you visually inspect your dog for any ticks. This means checking between the toes, in the ears, and under the tail. Keep an eye on ground conditions. Gravel can be very sharp. Fields can be full of broken glass and cans. Remember, your dog does not wear shoes, and his feet may not be up to the terrain. If the ground is too rough, you may wish to look into footwear for your Great Dane.

Finally, there needs to be a word about drinking and hydration. Always be sure your dog is drinking enough. It is easy to remember the need in the heat, but when it gets cold, dogs drink less. Be sure to keep track of how much moisture your dog is getting. The Centers for Disease Control and Prevention recommend not drinking cold water when overheated as abdominal cramping can occur. Instead, offer tepid or cool water. Move your dog to a cool, shaded spot. Cooler collars or blankets soaked in cool water over the body can also help. Should he be showing any signs of severe heat exhaustion (or heatstroke), follow the previous advice and get him medical attention immediately. Signs can include heavy panting, glassy eyes, staggering, and a red or purple tongue.

Danes on Wheels

When you plan to go farther than the neighborhood, you and your dog will need to be prepared for car travel. Remember, Great Danes have the same weight as a human passenger. He can suffer the same dangers and hazards as you. One way to keep him safe while driving is belting him into a seat. You can find a variety of such canine seat belts at pet supply stores, though his size may mean you have to find a mail order site. Consider that on long trips, this sort of restraint may not be ideal.

CAUTION

Transporting any size dog in the open bed of a pickup truck is extremely dangerous. According to the American Humane Society more than 100,000 dogs are killed each year by falling out of trucks. Though some manufacturers offer special harnesses, the size of a Great Dane makes most of these ineffective. If you must use the truck bed, be sure to keep your dog in a crate that is secured to the truck itself. Don't let your best friend become a roadside statistic.

Depending on the size of your vehicle, you may wish to have a crate for him to ride in. The crate should also be secured inside the vehicle. A tumbling or sliding crate can be as dangerous as a tumbling dog. Also of use are various auto barriers that put a divider between pets and the passengers. These can be a true lifesaver in sudden stops and turns.

Life Without a Leash

Unleashed areas can be great fun for you and your Great Dane. They also offer their own special demands. Although the majority of dogs in a leash-free area may behave, dogs still have a territorial pack ancestry that may rear its head in some situations. This is an activity that counts on him listening to you and following your commands. (A note of caution: Dogs that show any signs of aggression toward other animals or humans should never be taken to leash-free environments.)

When in leash-free zones, it is important to watch the body language of other dogs and owners as well as your own. You know your dog and should be aware of how he will react in various situations. You do not have any idea how other dogs will respond. Aside from noise (barking), you should keep an eye out for bristled back fur, extremely raised tails, and owners who look worried around their pets. This worry could be indicative of owners distressed about the safety of their pets or about how their pets may behave.

Once again, the size of the Great Dane plays a factor in leash-free areas. He will most likely be one of the biggest, if not the biggest, dog in the group. This can cause otherwise calm dogs to become forward and investigative.

Also, his size may intimidate other dog owners. At times the arrival of a Great Dane signals an exodus from the park of other dogs and owners. His size may make other owners nervous around their pets, which in turn can make their own dogs more nervous. A good start is to try to let your dog meet the other owners. Once they see how playful, happy, and gentle he is, the other owners will realize he most likely won't "eat" their little dog and they will relax.

It is important to balance the fun factor with the control factor. Usually this needs to be done only early in the session. Once the dogs have met and everyone has evaluated the personalities, often all will be fine. In fact, it can be comical to see your Great Dane parading around a leash-free park or beach with a string of smaller dogs following behind.

CAUTION

Leash-Free Park Worries

Many dog owners do not like the concept of dog parks and worry about the dangers of potential confrontations and fights. There are many folks who have horror stories of things that have happened at leash-free parks and beaches. But any time you are in a situation surrounded by strangers, problems can occur. Statistics show that most children's injuries occur at playgrounds. That may sound like a good argument to keep children and pets out of play areas, but the fact is that such play can be extremely positive. It is a choice every parent and owner must consider carefully.

Cross-Country Danes

If you are thinking of taking a longer trip and want to include your Great Dane, you will need to consider the following.

ACTIVITIES Thinking Outside the Park

Don't think you need to limit yourself and your Great Dane's outings to the dog park. He can be great fun in many settings. And a pet that is used to traveling and is well mannered can become a real adventurer.

- **Pet Supply Stores**—Many stores, independents and chains, allow leashed pets. He will enjoy looking over the various toys and treats as much as a child enjoys a trip to the toy store. There are now a number of dog-based snack companies (such as Three Dog Bakery) that allow you and your Great Dane to come in to pick out healthful treats.
- **City Streets and Strip Malls**—Taking him window-shopping down the street is not only good exercise, but also good for socialization. (See Chapter 3.) Such visits to town open up all kinds of possible experiences. For larger cities or more suburban areas, where downtowns are not quite as accessible, you could take him to one of the strip malls. Again, it gives you both something new to look at while walking.
- **Renaissance and Street Fairs**—Many Renaissance fairs will allow you to bring leashed pets. Some members of the fair really love the involvement of such a large dog. You may also wish to consider small community events, church events, and holiday fairs that allow pets, as all are wonderful opportunities to bond with your Great Dane.

Always travel with his medical history. Many boarding facilities (even at Disneyland) require proof of vaccinations should you desire to stay there. A simple rabies tag or dog license may not be enough. Some now insist on seeing an actual shots record. If you do not have one, be certain to keep your veterinarian's phone number and fax number with you at all times.

Be certain your overnight destinations are large-pet friendly. Although a hotel may say it is pet friendly, many define an approved pet as "less than 25 pounds." Your boy will have topped that by the time he is around 10 weeks old! When checking into a hotel, always ask for a ground-level floor to make potty breaks more convenient. Should you be stuck on a higher floor, a bathtub can become a place for emergency bathroom needs with a young

Breed Truths

Tail Lengths

Because of the length of their tail, many Great Danes may find it awkward to sit. Their tail can get bent in an uncomfortable position under their hindquarters. It may be easier and more comfortable for many Great Danes to lie down than to sit.

SHOPPING LIST

First Aid Kit

When on the road, or even at home, a canine first aid kit is a good idea. Though everybody and every Great Dane has specific needs, basics in a kit should include the following items:

- Simethicone gas pills
- Benadryl pills (for allergies from plants or stings)
- Pepto-Bismol or Maalox (antidiarrheal)
- Scissors
- Sports tape
- Veterinary wrap
- Bandage materials
- Sterile saline wash for wounds (like Vet-Aid)

puppy. Having a crate in tow will allow him to rest at night and even spend a bit of safe alone time should you need to leave the room.

Take things he will want and need. If he has a favorite toy or blanket, bring them along for security. If he is on a special diet, bring plenty of his special food. You may not always be able to find it at a local store. If he is fed a raw diet, a cooler will keep food fine between grocery stops. Also, bring any medications he is on or may need should there be an emergency.

Should you go on a trip where you cannot bring him along, be certain he is well cared for in your absence. Beside the standard kennels and pet hotels, you might look into a licensed and bonded pet sitter. In any of these situations, be certain there are written instructions on what to do should he need any sort of medical help. You may also wish to give a figure of how much you are willing to spend on any such emergency. Obviously, if possible find a location you can contact regularly to check in on your friend.

The Good Citizen

The American Kennel Club has a standardized test to certify that your Great Dane will be a good ambassador to the breed. It is called the Canine Good Citizen (CGC) program. The CGC test is a preset series of ten separate challenges. If he completes all 10 challenges, he will earn a Canine Good Citizenship certificate.

The test is relatively simple if he already knows basic commands. While taking the test, your Great Dane should not be shy, aggressive, or resentful. (Of note: Before taking the actual evaluation, be sure to potty your dog. If he urinates or defecates during the test, it is an immediate disqualification.)

Per the AKC, the 10 parts are as follows:

1. Accepting a friendly stranger
2. Sitting politely for petting
3. Appearance and grooming
4. Out for a walk (walking on a loose lead)
5. Walking through a crowd
6. *Sit* and *down* on command and staying in place
7. Coming when called
8. Reaction to another dog
9. Reaction to distraction
10. Supervised separation

All the tasks are performed on-lead.

The Canine Good Citizenship certification is a grand start, as it can help you prepare for doing more with your Great Dane. You can contact the American Kennel Club to find out when and where the next tests in your area will be (*www.AKC.org*).

Sport Competitions

Perhaps you and your Great Dane would be interested in getting into sports. There is a wide variety of group events to choose from. Some require skill, some training, and some physical attributes. Based on your schedule and desires, the two of you may try one or more.

Agility

One activity you and your Great Dane may wish to check into is agility. The history of agility may be traced to the 1970s in the United Kingdom, where dogs were run through a jumping course, similar to one a horse might do, as a way to entertain the audience at a large dog show.

Today agility is a timed obstacle course designed more as a sport. It still features jumps but also weave poles, teeter-totters, tunnels, and more. What a sight it is to see a Great Dane compact himself and breeze through a tunnel!

Before 18 months of age Great Danes should not attempt obstacles with heavy impacts for their safety. Jumps, teeter-totters, and similar tasks can damage the growth of his bones and joints. If desired, you can begin training on lower-impact tasks like weave poles, tunnels, chutes, and walking a plank on the ground (to prepare for later elevated walks).

As long as your goal is to have fun with your dog, agility can be a great activity. Several organizations, including the American Kennel Club, the United Kennel Club, the North American Dog Agility Council, and the United States Dog Agility Association, sponsor trials and award titles, each with slightly different styles of agility. A look at these groups' websites will give more information on this fun, fast-paced sport.

Obedience

Should you and your Great Dane decide to try a more challenging course, there is traditional obedience. According to the AKC, "Demonstrating the usefulness of a dog as a companion to humankind, AKC Obedience is a sport with rules, regulations, judges, conditioning, training, placements, and prizes. Dog and handler teams are judged on how closely they match the judge's mental picture of a theoretically perfect performance as they execute a series of specified exercises. Accuracy and precision are essential, but the natural movement of the handler and the willingness and enjoyment of the dog are very important." The obedience excercises were created in 1933 by Helen Whitehouse Walker, who wanted to show the intelligence of her Poodles. The first AKC trial was in 1936 and featured 200 dogs!

The AKC actually has three levels of obedience: Novice, Open, and Utility. Tests for the novice level include Heel on Leash and Figure Eight, Stand for Examination, Recall, Long Sit, and Long Down. For Open they add such tests as Drop on Recall, Retrieve on Flat, and Broad Jump. Utility is the most complex, with such tests as Scent Discrimination, Directed Retrieve, and Directed Jumping. To get through these tests, you and your Great Dane must train steadily and have a true connection.

For more on AKC Obedience check out their website, *www.akc.org/events/obedience*

Fun Facts

There is quite a debate about whether Great Danes should be classified as working dogs even though they were once referred to as boarhounds. Despite resembling a hound in many ways, the American Kennel Club, which categorizes breeds in the United States according to their function, has placed the Great Dane into the working dog group as opposed to the hound group.

Rally

If you and your Great Dane love to work together on tricks and commands, rally may be for you. Rally obedience is a sport where you both go through a series of preset commands. As the two of you walk a designated course, you come to signs; each has instructions telling you which task to perform. Some are moving exercises (*heel, turn, circle,* and so on), whereas others are stationary exercises (such as *lie down* and *stay*). In the Beginning or Novice class, he is on-lead. In the more advanced classes your dog is off-lead. Unlike traditional obedience, in rally you can talk as much as you want to your dog and repeat commands. In the beginning of the course every dog starts off with a score of 100 points, and points are deducted only for mistakes that the judge notices.

Rally is a great sport for you and your dog because it's fairly low-key and really fun. And if you work at it, your Great Dane can earn a number of titles. To find out more about the commands, the signs, and the challenges, check out *www.rallyobedience.com*.

Tracking

Great Danes were initially bred to hunt wild boar. Though the breed is more like a sight hound than a scent hound, some do exhibit a strong scent base. Should yours enjoy using his nose to find objects, you might consider getting involved with tracking through specific American Kennel Club sanctioned shows.

To discover if your dog is motivated, you can try a couple of tracking games. The easiest is to hide snacks around the room while he is out of sight. Let him in and see how quickly and completely he locates all the treats. A keen nose can find them in drawers, under items, and even next to other smelly objects such as shoes. If your dog is enjoying the activity, and is good at it, you may wish to move up to doing actual tracking. You can get more information at *www.akc.org/events/tracking*.

Fun Facts

Junior Handling

Shows can also be a family event. Some shows offer a Junior Handling class where youngsters can be in the ring with their own dog. This is a class where the dog's structure, color, or even being spayed or neutered are of no concern, as it is the child (handler) being judged. The time a child spends training and working with a dog can build great character.

Conformation

Conformation is probably the best-known dog competition. If you have seen the Westminster Kennel Club dog show (in the United States) or Crufts (in Great Britain) on TV, you are familiar with the various breeds trotting about the ring and being examined by the judge. Each breed is judged against a published breed standard; the dog that is closest in the judge's opinion to its breed standard wins. See page 149 for information on the Great Dane standard. This is what conformation is all about.

FYI: U.S. Dog Show Organizations

In the United States, there are three main dog show organizations

- The American Kennel Club—AKC. This is the group that most people think of when they talk of dog shows. Originating in 1884, it is their standards that most U.S. breeders try to adhere to. The American Kennel Club, perhaps best known for conformation (the look, structure, and movement of the dog), also offer activities such as obedience and agility at various shows. This is the organization that holds well-known shows, including the yearly televised Westminster Dog Show and the Eukanuba National Championship.
- The United Kennel Club—UKC. This group, founded in 1898, bases its judging on more than just looks. It also judges performance. Their shows feature conformation but can also host activities from weight pulls to night hunts to dock diving. The United Kennel Club also focuses on the bond between owner and dog by not allowing professional handlers (someone paid to show dogs) to be used at their events.
- The International All Breed Canine Association—IABCA. This organization has been in existence since the late 1980s. It was formed to allow dogs in the United States a chance to obtain the International UCI Championship Title. The UCI (Union Cynologie International) was formed in Germany during the 1970s. A key difference is that dogs do not compete against each other in an International All Breed Canine Association show for their titles, and the judge gives a written evaluation on each entry.

This is easily the most difficult and maybe the most frustrating of all competitions, because unlike agility, obedience, and rally, which are based on following rules, conformation is based strictly on opinion. It is not unusual at a multiday dog show for a dog to be seen the best by one judge and then totally dismissed by another judge the following day.

For a better idea of show life, check with the American Kennel Club, United Kennel Club, or International All Breed Canine Association for local shows in your area and attend a few. (These three U.S. groups all have different takes on how to run shows.) Talk with those who show to get a well-rounded idea of what the show life is like. The organizations' websites will also contain lots of information on rules, fees, restrictions, and so on, allowing you to decide which group you may want to start with.

One other source to check is your Great Dane. After all, he is the one who has to be groomed, taken, and made to wait all day to show, and then be paraded around in a ring. Although some dogs seem to live for it, others are obviously not interested, and appear bored or may find it distressing. If he is not interested in showing, it is unlikely he will look "good" in the ring.

Perhaps the biggest fact to remember is that dog shows are like contests. As the legal language on most contests say, "Many will enter. Few will win."

FYI: Therapy or Service?

There are two official designations for animals that officially aid humans: "therapy" animals and "service" animals. The service animal is the most well known because of the many stories about guide dogs and such. Therapy animals are equally important, as they bring joy and comfort to people in places such as hospitals and nursing homes. The legal difference is that therapy animals must be invited into any location that does not normally allow animals, whereas service animals, by law, can enter any place their human can.

You can attend shows for months and never even place in a class. If you are not chosen for a prize at a dog show, it does not necessarily mean your Great Dane does not have the right stuff. It simply means a judge chose a different dog. Just be sure you never allow disappointment to enter your mind. Your Great Dane will sense it and feel he has let you down. As long as you look to conformation, or any sport, as an event to share with him, win or lose, the two of you will have fun.

Great Danes for Therapy

Great Danes, with their gentle spirits and massive size, can offer a great deal of love. Your Great Dane may be able to share that love with people who do not have an opportunity to enjoy canine companionship on a regular basis. Registered therapy pets and their owners visit nursing homes and hospitals. These visits can bring a great deal of joy.

To qualify as a therapy dog, he will need to be comfortable around people, take commands, and remain stable no matter what he comes across. Generally, if a dog is able to receive a Canine Good Citizen certification, it is likely he can pass the test for therapy pet acceptance.

Therapy dogs need to enjoy meeting people. They need to be comfortable around things found in hospitals such as wheelchairs, slick floors, therapy rooms, and electronic equipment. This is definitely not a job for a Great Dane that is nervous, shy, or aloof.

Helpful Hints

How to Get Registered

There are a variety of groups that can test and register therapy dogs. These include Therapy Dogs International (*www.tdi-dog.org*) and the Delta Society (*www.deltasociety.org*). However, there are many other organizations that can offer registration and certification such as Love on a Leash (*www.loveonaleash.org*). Check for local group chapters near you.

Leash Training

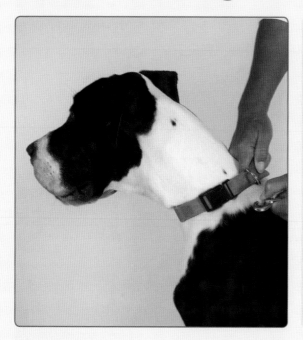

1 Place a collar on your Great Dane and attach a leash. Praise him.

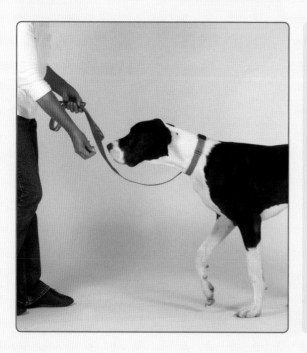

2 Move away from him a small distance and call to him. As he moves toward you, praise and reward him with a treat. Repeat until he begins to walk along with you. Continue to praise and occasionally reward.

3 If he tries to go in different directions, stops and rears, or pulls back in an attempt to free himself from the collar, move in his direction a few steps before trying to guide him your way again. If he refuses to move, try to change his focus with a toy, a bit of noise, or a distraction. Then see if he'll walk back with you to someplace he wants to go.

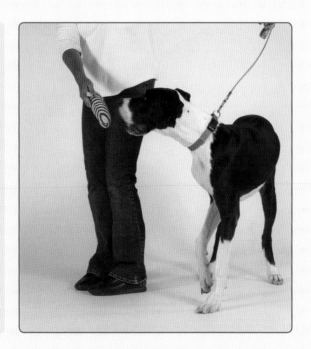

4 As the training progresses, you can ignore him when he occasionally stops. But be sure to praise as soon as he lets the leash go slack.

The Sit Command

1 Stand in front of your Great Dane. Hold a treat or object just above his eyes. Move the treat higher and back. As he begins to squat, say *"Sit!"* Follow with a treat.

2 Now hold the treat almost behind his sight line over his head. Repeat the *sit!* command as you are moving it behind him. When his bottom hits the ground, reward with praise and a treat.

3 With no treat, guide with only your hand. As his bottom lowers, say *"Sit."* After he has sat, give him praise and a treat.

4 As he progresses, use a hand signal with the verbal command. After each successful *sit*, praise and reward.

The Stay Command

1 Have your Great Dane stand in front of you. Look at him and firmly say *"Stay"* as you put your hand out in a "stop" signal. Be careful not to startle him. Quickly praise, reward, and then release him—*release* meaning that the task is over.

2 Repeat the process. After several successes, step backward, away from him. You may want to repeat the *stay* command. Always praise and reward him before you give him the release word.

3 Begin moving in various directions. Turn your back to him. Walk around him. The key is to have him remain still while you do another activity.

4 Once you can move around him without a problem, try dropping the verbal command and use just the hand signal. Also begin using the command at various locations.

Chapter Eight

Grooming a Great Dane

Great Danes, despite their size, are a fairly easy breed to keep looking good. Often referred to as a "wash-and-wear" breed, their short coat is easily lathered and rinsed. Only when show purposes require special needs can the work get a tad more complex, particularly on Great Danes with large amounts of white on them.

Big-Dog Bathing

Bathing is about the only major grooming activity you will need to do with your Great Dane. His hair will gather oil and dirt. With the occasional bath, he will not only have a cleaner coat, but a softer, better-smelling coat, making him more appealing to snuggle.

During warm weather you may wash him outdoors using a bucket or two of warm water. The bucket(s) are for wetting and the first rinse after lathering up. Use a hose for the final rinse. When performing the task outside, be sure to have full control of him. Otherwise he may run off to roll on the ground and you will need to start all over again! Also it's not a good idea to wash him on dirt or your lawn, as mud can defeat the purpose.

Hair Care

The Great Dane sports a short-haired coat that requires little grooming. Though not a shaggy dog, your Great Dane will shed almost continually. Most notable will be his white hair, which seems to end up every place.

To help remove dead hair, a soft rubber-toothed curry comb, rubber-toothed grooming glove, or a grooming block will be your best grooming tools. If you spend just a few minutes a day brushing, you will see a marked difference in the amount of hair found around the house and in your vacuum cleaner. Not only does it remove the hair, but he will enjoy the massage.

FYI: Washing a Big Dog

Bathing a large breed is akin to washing a full-sized human. It will not be easy to maneuver him around during the process. You may even opt to do it outdoors. Below are steps in the process.

Prepare:
- If he is allowed on furniture, place clean, dry blankets on your (his) couch or bed, for he may head for these areas when the bath is done.
- Safety note: If using a bathtub, have no-slip decals in place to help him keep his footing.
- Mix up a solution of shampoo and warm water; a little will go a long way. You can put this solution in a bowl, or for more convenience a squirt bottle.

Wash:
- Wet him all over. A handheld detachable showerhead will make things faster and easier.
- Try to keep him from shaking. Not only will this wet all the surroundings, but it may cause him to lose his balance . . . and yours too. One method is to keep one hand on his neck and shoulder region.
- Pour the shampoo mixture on him and work it into a lather with your hand. Also useful are a washcloth, a sponge, a shower scrunchie, or even a rubber curry comb.
- Use a washcloth around his face and ears, and in the folds of his lips.
- Rinse him down from head to tail, top to bottom.

Dry:
- Letting him shake is a good start. (You may want to hold a towel in front of yourself.)
- Do a quick towel-dry before he makes a break for your couch or bed. You can also use a horse sweat scraper to remove excess water before towel drying.
- On cold days, be sure he has a place to rest and keep warm.

Repeat:
- Just kidding.

A grooming block is a man-made pumice-like substance. It works by catching the dead hair in its pores and gently pulling them out. This stone is commonly used on livestock such as horses and cattle. To use the block, you rub it at an angle, pulling downward. Some say it works like a magnet for dead hair. Many breeders use it during shows when their Great Dane is shedding heavily.

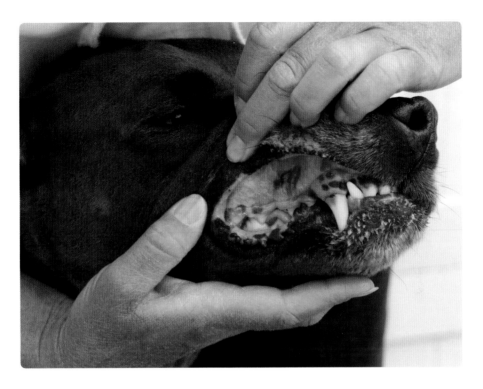

Great Danes and the Dentist

A puppy typically has 28 teeth, whereas the average adult will have 42. Great Dane puppies start to lose their baby teeth as early as three months of age. Most teeth fall out on their own accord while eating or during play. Yet in some cases they remain, even though a permanent tooth is growing in. It is not a concern for a few days, but if the baby tooth remains for a week or more, it may need to be extracted by a veterinarian.

To help your Great Dane's pearly whites, you can begin with dental care when he is just a puppy. There are a variety of devices, from standard-looking toothbrushes to brushes you slip on your finger. Also available is toothpaste made just for dogs, which often comes in meat-based flavors for your dog's enjoyment. If you prefer, you can use just water. It is ideal to brush his teeth once a day. Plaque buildup can lead to more serious problems. Other than brushing his choppers, you may wish to consider products that

Breed Truths

Tooth Count

Although most Great Danes have a total of 42 adult teeth, some may be missing teeth. This in itself is no cause for alarm, as they are often small pre-molars, which have little effect. However, it may mean you need to be extra careful with your Great Dane's dental care program, as teeth near the vacant spot may develop uneven wear or possibly an increase of tartar buildup.

dissolve plaque buildup by altering the mouth pH in hopes of preventing the need for professional cleaning. Note: Never use human toothpaste, as it is not made to be ingested and could make him feel ill.

The most common problem from plaque is tartar. Allowed to spread, tartar can lead to periodontal disease. This can cause tooth loss and bacteria enter the bloodstream and attack the organs. Giving him a large raw (not cooked) soup bone may help him clean his own teeth. The chewing action and extra saliva help break down tartar. (Always monitor heavy chewing, as tooth damage could occur.) If plagued with tartar he may need to have it removed by a veterinarian. If that is necessary, ask if the work can be done without anesthesia.

Ear Care

Whether their ears are natural or cropped, Great Danes have large ear canals. These canals can easily trap dust and moisture. If you have multiple dogs, it is possible that they will keep each other's ears clean. Though that certainly can help, you will have to be in charge of ear maintenance.

Breed Truths

Ears Up or Down

Some say that drop ears or ears that hang down have more problems than those that are upright or cropped. This belief is not supported by research. Dogs (and breeds) in general with floppy ears are no more susceptible to ear infections than those with erect ears. Ear infections are more likely influenced by environment, diet, hygiene, the dog's own body chemistry, and his immune system than the position of the ears themselves.

If he has excessive sludge, use an ear cleanser such as K9 Ear Solution or Nolvasan Otic. For a more holistic approach there are a number of brands that use tea tree oil, which may help soothe irritated ears.

Squeeze a bit of solution into the ear. Gently massage the base of the ear to help work the liquid downward. At this time, he may lean his head toward your hand and begin to moan deeply. Once you stop, allow him to shake his head a couple of times. Excessive head shaking can lead to damage of the ear leather (flaps). Next take a cotton ball or cloth and gently wipe out the residue. Should the ears appear red, swollen, warmer than usual to the touch, or painful, a veterinary visit is called for, as he could have an infection.

If you see what looks like black grit or sand in his ear, he may have ear mites. Ear mites are common, and can be gotten from other cats or dogs. They are usually pretty easily gotten rid of with treatments from your veterinarian. Left untreated, mites can cause hearing loss and possible damage to the ear from habitual scratching.

Besides being annoying, excessive scratching of the ears and shaking of the head may result in a thickening of part of the ear flap, whether ears are cropped or not. This thickening, called a hematoma, is actually a buildup or pooling of blood. A hematoma in a cropped ear may affect the way the ear stands or could even prevent it from standing at all. If your dog develops an ear hematoma, you may want to take him to the veterinarian. Hematomas can be more than just a cosmetic issue and may obstruct the ear canal and lead to future problems.

Pedicures

Great Danes have huge feet, and thus have large nails. These nails can unintentionally injure a person should your dog step on your bare foot or jump up. It can be a regular "nightmare on Dane's feet." Not only can these nails hurt others, but they can be harmful to him, as they could affect his gait, possibly causing pain or lameness. If he has overgrown dewclaws (thumbs of his front legs), they could get caught on crates or fences and possibly torn off.

For trimming a Great Dane's nails, a non-guillotine type of nail clippers (which look a bit like wire cutters) is easy to use. Be sure any nail-trimming device is sharp. You can also try a sanding tool or similar nail grinder, but be sure not to let it overheat the nail.

Have him lie down. This gives you better control of his feet. Before starting, look for the root of the nail, called the quick. This is a sensitive part of the nail, and if you cut it, it may cause pain and bleed. The quick is quite visible in light colored nails, but in dark-colored ones it can be much harder to locate.

While trimming nails it is a good idea to cradle his foot in your left hand (if you are left handed, hold it in your right). An adult dog's paw more than likely will completely fill your hand. Holding the nail clippers in your right hand, slide the opening of the clippers over just the pointed tip of his nail. Once comfortable with the placement make a quick cutting motion with a squeeze of your hand. Trim the right and then left edge off the sides of the nail to shape it. These edges you trim from the underside of the paw almost appear hollow. Continue to repeat on the nails on all his paws. If you choose, smooth down any rough edges with a sanding tool.

Unfortunately, some Great Danes may seem to think you are not only trimming their nails, but cutting off their toes. Patience, praise, and treats can go a long way, but training at a young age will not only help make it easier to do but will also help his nails stay shorter in the long run.

Flea and Parasite Wars

A major part of grooming is keeping your Great Dane free of fleas. In some areas where it is extremely cold or at a high elevation, fleas are less common. But for many owners, fleas will be a constant issue.

Fighting Fleas Naturally

A natural, chemical-free, nontoxic approach to getting rid of fleas is to use human-grade diatomaceous earth, commonly referred to as DE. DE is a powder consisting of finely ground micro-skeletons of a type of deceased algae called diatoms. Sprinkling DE on pets and carpets will cause fleas to die from dehydration. Even though DE is nontoxic, it is best not to breathe the powder in. When applying DE, you should wear a mask and place a washcloth over the end of your Great Dane's muzzle. Once the powder has settled, it will be safe. (It is safe enough to be approved by the U.S. Department of Agriculture as a feed additive.)

Sprinkle some DE powder on your Great Dane's spine. Massage it along the body, working your way to his legs and paws. Avoid contact with the eyes. When using DE on carpet, sprinkle it on, brush it in, then vacuum in five to seven days to get rid of dead or dying fleas. Repeat as necessary. (NOTE: Do not use DE meant for swimming pools. Use only human-grade DE.)

As fleas are known for disliking the taste of garlic and yeast, another form of flea control may be to mix these two items with your Great Dane's food or give as supplements. Be aware that some dogs may be yeast intolerant, which may result in a skin allergy. If this is the case, discontinue use. Though some studies throw doubt on the effectiveness of this system, many veterinarians still recommend the regimen.

Fun Facts

Make Up!

Great Danes are no strangers to makeup. Many times, they are made up to meet the needs of a film appearance. For example, in the movie The Patriot (starring Mel Gibson), a Harlequin Great Dane (named Vanilla Fudge) is painted to look like a Mantle. There are also cases where multiple dogs need to play the same character so various tricks are used to make them all look alike. And many a Great Dane has been made up as the horrible Hound of the Baskervilles for more than one filmed version of the Sherlock Holmes tale.

But beyond Hollywood, Great Danes are sometimes given a visual boost at conformation dog shows. One of the more common artistic procedures is the use of black markers to cover scarring or premature gray in black areas. Hair dye is another popular way to cover up gray. (It's not just for people!) White chalk, baby powder, or cornstarch is often used to brighten white areas that may seem dingy or to aid in covering rusty saliva stains. However, it should be noted that all dyes and foreign substances are illegal in many show rings such as those sponsored by the AKC and the UKC. The use of them are grounds for disqualification.

Still another natural repellent is apple cider vinegar (ACV), which can be given in the form of a pill or added directly to drinking water. ACV makes the blood less favorable to biting insects—not only fleas but mosquitoes as well. A number of veterinarians and health care specialists also believe ACV can help strengthen the immune system. The best ACV to use is one that is unfiltered so it contains the most beneficial enzymes.

Chemical Warfare

A quicker and more direct attack can be performed with commonly used flea products. Many of these chemical killers can be purchased from your veterinarian. As with all chemicals, caution should be taken, as they have a potential to be toxic or may lead to unexpected side effects. This toxicity may result from unexpected sensitivity or accidental overdose. Possible side effects are vomiting, diarrhea, loss of appetite, weakness, lethargy, drooling, or odd behavior. Adverse reactions may occur immediately to several days after application. If a topical treatment renders an immediate reaction, try to thoroughly rinse it off.

Before using any chemical, be sure to check the labels. Most flea treatments are not recommended for pregnant, debilitated, geriatric, or nursing animals, or puppies under eight weeks of age. Many of the labels suggest that you consult with your veterinarian before use. Below is a list of the nine most common flea-killing chemicals.

- Amitraz—found in Zema and Promeris (kills ticks for up to one month)
- Fipronil—found in Frontline (kills fleas and possibly ticks for one to three months)
- Imidacloprid—found in Advantix and Advantage (kills fleas for one month)
- Lufenuron—found in Program (renders fleas that bite the dog sterile)
- Metaflumizone—found in Promeris (kills fleas for one month)
- Nitenpyram—found in Capstar (kills fleas in 30 minutes; no residual action)
- Permethrin—found in Advantix, Bio Spot, Precor2000, and Zodiac (kills fleas, and to a lesser extent, ticks; no residual action)
- Pyriproxifen—found in Micodex (renders fleas that bite the dog sterile)
- Selamectin—found in Revolution (kills fleas, prevents heartworms)

Ticks

Ticks are spider-looking bloodsuckers that get under your skin and your Great Dane's too. There are many products that aid in controlling them, but you should know how to handle ticks should you find them.

Ticks are often on branches and leaves of bushes, hoping to catch a ride on passing animals. After visiting an area that may have had ticks, be certain to fully inspect your Great Dane. Ticks tend to like crevices and areas with little to no hair, such as ears, between toes, and in the groin and armpit regions. If you find a tick, use a latex glove (if you have one—at the least a tissue).

Grasp the tick close to the skin without squeezing it. Pull it straight out or use a specially designed tick-removal tool if on hand.

Once it is removed, you may want to save the tick in a small container like a pill vial or jar with a bit of rubbing alcohol in it, just in case future illness occurs. This way the tick can be identified if needed. Ticks are equal-opportunity pests, so be sure to inspect the human members of your party also.

Mites

All dogs have a few mites on their skin. In puppies, the immune system may not be strong enough and the mites can grow at a rapid rate. Mites can cause severe irritations by tunneling through hair follicles into the skin, causing excessive itching and hair loss. Mites in canines are generally known as mange. Topical treatments usually solve the problem.

There are actually several types of mange.

- Demodectic mange, sometimes called demodex, is the most common form of mange. It comes from a mite that lives in hair follicles. Under the microscope it resembles an alligator with eight legs!
- Sarcoptic mange, commonly called canine scabies, is an intensely itchy disorder that even humans can catch. You will see it on your Great Dane as small bumps and crusts on the ear tips, abdomen, elbows, and hocks. This condition can be treated with shampoos and topical medications. Side effects to sarcoptic mange are bacterial infections and even yeast infections.

Chapter Nine

The Senior Great Dane

A Great Dane's life span is often regarded as short. Their life expectancy is 7 to 10 years. But they will give so much love in that time. As the years go by, you may notice your Great Dane is becoming a senior citizen, or veteran, often around six years of age. As with people, each body ages differently, some more visibly than others. Though older, and perhaps wiser, he will still be able to share his life with you. You just need to realize that his needs will change as he ages.

The Golden Years

Great Danes continue their big-dog ways well into their senior years; they just might not have as much energy or ability. You can expect him to continue wanting to be part of the family and wanting to do all the things he has regularly done.

As age takes its toll on his body and mind, it will be up to you to be sure that such changes do not damage his spirit. The Great Dane has a strong sense of pride and honor. He may actually show remorse if he feels he cannot keep up with your demands or his past abilities. Praise him for the things he can do. Help him when you can. And whenever possible, let him do things. It may take him a bit longer to do it alone, but he will feel better about himself afterward.

Keep him active. A well-known law of physics is that items that are in motion tend to remain in motion. Even though he may want to be sleeping more during the day, get him up and moving regularly. Even though he may want to resist activity because of some arthritic stiffness or pain, keep coaxing him to get up and walk around the house, the yard, and so on. Walk with him, but do not make the pace one that he needs to struggle with.

Let him play, but keep the pace and needs lower. Do not toss things as far for fetch. If you have several dogs, make sure he has a safe haven to keep from being trampled in the crowd. A dog cot is a great place to let him rest and still maintain some height among the group. (Often a senior Great Dane will bark happily as other dogs wrestle around him as his way of being included.)

Make sure his mind stays active. Do not keep him away from family members. He will often find it more pleasurable to be around his family and seeing them interact. But know when he needs his space too. Hide some treats nearby for him to find. Teach him simple tricks he can do while lying down. And above all, talk to him, though there will be times he may be tired and not up to a lot of socialization. On those days, let him rest.

Since his energy levels are lower, long trips and tasks may become unpleasant. As legs stiffen, long walks, stairs, boarding vehicles, and so on may become a challenge for your Great Dane. Be certain to gauge any event you and he attend and have his needs in mind. For example, will the weather be extremely hot or cold? Will there be someplace comfortable for him to lie or rest? Will the length of the trip be excessive compared with the fun he will have? Remember, he will still want to please you and attempt any trip or task you want. It will be up to you to be certain that your Great Dane will not feel he has let you down.

Also note that older dogs have less ability to regulate body heat. They get chilled or overheated much more easily than when they were younger. Be sure to have plenty of blankets in cold weather. If you see him curled up, or if he feels cool to the touch, it usually indicates he is chilly. Place a blanket over him to cover his chest and rear end. In a short time, you will often see him stretch out a bit. Similarly, in hot weather, be certain you have a fan that can be used to help cool him. A cool, damp towel can also be helpful on extremely warm days.

The Aging Body

Perhaps the most noticeable changes in canines as they age are the same as those in humans. These are mostly related to lessening of the senses and agility. Your Great Dane should handle most of these changes calmly.

Stiffness and Arthritis

Arthritis strikes older canines like it does humans, causing pain and stiffness in joints. One way to help your senior Great Dane is to watch his weight. A heavier body can unnecessarily create more discomfort. You can help maintain his weight and lessen arthritis with moderate exercise, like walking, once or twice a day.

Supplements can be another way to treat arthritis. Supplements such as those containing glucosamine, chondroitin sulfate, MSM, and hylaronic acid may help, as they aid in repairing the body to decrease the pain of arthritis. Other things that may help are items rich in omega-3 fatty acids. Sources include fish oil and some vegetable oils such as canola, olive, or flaxseed.

Another thing to consider is giving him Duralactin, which is a compound made from the milk of grass-fed cows that has anti-inflammatory properties. Duralactin is available without a prescription, and often comes in a palatable pill scented and flavored with vanilla.

If all else fails, don't be afraid to ask your veterinarian about medications to reduce pain. After all, you want your best friend to have quality of life.

Hip Muscle Loss

Giant breeds are susceptible to hip problems at any age. But as they age, they begin to lose muscle tone in their hindquarters. This can cause the dog's rear end to lose a bit of coordination and possibly shake as he walks. It may make it difficult for him to lift a leg to urinate. He may have trouble getting up from a *sit* or *down* position. Stairs may become hard to navigate. When this begins, there is little to be done except to try to keep him moving. You will also want to start altering some of his habits and begin avoiding stairs and guide him away from beds or anything that requires him to jump. Or better yet, if possible, add or find an easier, safer way to get there.

The Loss of Sight and Sound

Great Danes do not often reach an age where vision or hearing loss becomes a problem. However, like humans, dogs can lose these senses at any age because of injuries or illness. They can also be born blind or deaf, a common issue with white Great Danes.

For those that do develop age-related vision problems, you may start to notice a slight haziness when you look into the pupil (black part) of his eye. That is normal, and does not affect vision much. However, if it becomes very gray or even white, he probably has cataracts. If desired a canine ophthalmologist can remove the lens and even replace it with an artificial lens, just like humans get.

FYI: Senior Great Dane Comfort & Caution Tips

As your Great Dane ages, here are some tips to help him along.

- Put a blanket on him when it is cold, if he seems cool to the touch, or if he is balled up. This extra heat may make his joints feel better and move more easily.
- If he is no longer very mobile, he should change position every few hours at least. Help reposition him if he needs assistance. Not only can this keep his muscles from cramping up, but it can help prevent pressure sores.
- If he is weak in the rear, using a soft beach towel under his belly as a sling and carefully lifting up can help him get to his feet.

And keep an eye on his "output."

- Watch his waste, both urine and fecal, keeping an eye on quantity, consistency, color, odor, and frequency.
- Changes in these could indicate the need to see your veterinarian.

Great Danes with hearing problems can be taught using signals by hand or light. If age issues are involved, the ability to hear high-pitched sounds usually goes first. Should this occur, try to call out in a lower tone of voice. If he has lost all hearing, be certain to stimulate him in other ways like petting. You do not want him to think you are not talking to him anymore. Also, you may consider looking into a vibration collar. (See page 70.)

Cognitive Dysfunction Syndrome

As your Great Dane ages, you may notice some behavioral changes that could be signs of cognitive dysfunction syndrome (CDS), also known as doggie Alzheimer's syndrome. This condition appears in elderly dogs and cats. A study of 139 elderly dogs at the University of California at Davis found that 62 percent had at least one major symptom.

Symptoms for CDS include forgetting how to walk up stairs, no longer greeting family members, more daytime sleeping, staring blankly at walls, wagging the tail differently, barking more at night for no apparent reason, and even growing aggression or separation anxiety. Eventually, the dog may not recognize any family members. If these are not being caused by some other medical condition, they could be signs of CDS.

Researchers believe that CDS is caused by plaques that form in the brain similar to those found in Alzheimer's patients. There are various chemical changes affecting brain activity. CDS also appears with higher levels of aluminum in the brain, which can also be seen in the dog's saliva. Treatment can include prescription medications. Some treat it with holistic and dietary means. At least one treatment consists of changing to a raw diet using mostly organic foods to lessen the ingestion of heavy metals.

Caring for the Elder Dane

Feeding

Older Great Danes may require shifts in their diets as their body and organs begin to age, just as humans need to alter diet as age increases. The liver and intestines can become less effective, making some foods harder to digest. The metabolism slows, allowing weight gain. At the same time, muscle tone can begin to diminish, causing weight loss.

In some ways, feeding your older Great Dane is similar to feeding him when he was a puppy. You have to be vigilant in watching his body, temperament, and waste for signs of need. His appetite may shift. His weight may shift. His tastes may even shift. His feces and urine may change color or texture. All of these must be noted and taken into consideration. You will want to adjust the types of food, the amount, and the feeding schedule as often as his eating habits suggest. Should he get slow to eat, sometimes just hand-offering him pieces of his meal may get him to start eating.

Constipation

Just like in older humans, constipation can occur in your Great Dane. This can cause him to feel uncomfortable and possibly be a precursor to other abdominal upsets.

At any age it is a good idea to keep an eye on his stools, but when he is a senior, it is especially important to know he is eliminating waste. Should you be concerned that things are a bit backed up, you may want to give your dog a few simethicone gas pills to aid in the discomfort of gas pressure. Be sure he is drinking and is well hydrated.

If he will eat it, you may choose to offer him several tablespoons of canned pumpkin. The fiber can help push things through. You can try a bit of mineral oil on your dog's food. (Around 1 teaspoon per 25 pounds of weight will do it.) Depending on the mobility of the dog, having him walk or walking with him will help stimulate stool movement. If walking is difficult, try a vibrating massage tool on his hindquarters and abdomen if he'll allow it. It will not only aid in relaxing muscles and possibly easing some of his arthritis, but its vibrations may help loosen his bowels. As a last resort, give him a warm-water enema. A large bulb syringe is the best tool for use, and is easily located at most drugstores or pharmacies.

Should the above not get the ball rolling, a call to your veterinarian is in order.

Grooming

An older Great Dane does not need any additional grooming because of age. But he also does not require any less. Grooming him in the golden years is more than just to keep up looks. It is a great time to check for early signs of problems related to aging.

While brushing, be sure to go over his skin with the palm of your hand to seek out any new or growing lumps. Many canines develop "age bumps" (usually fatty cysts), so they are not an immediate cause for alarm unless they seem to be rapidly growing in size or multiplying. Check toes for sores and short or bleeding nails. This could be the result of feet dragging, because of mobility problems. If you find any, consider getting him booties. Inspect his ears and mouth for signs of infection, tooth wear, or unusual bumps or marks. And give his body firm rubs and gently stretch out his legs to check for any possible soreness or pressure points.

A Great Dane has weight to him, so even though he may lie on soft bedding and furniture, he may develop "angry elbows." The skin on the joints can appear red, irritated, and even enlarged. A daily treatment of the area with ointments may help. If possible, rotate between two salves—a petroleum/lanolin-based one (like Bag Balm) on one day, and a tea tree oil compound (like Trainer's Formula) on alternate days.

As with humans, the aging process brings on odd bumps, skin conditions (spotting, for example), soreness, gray hair, and more. All of these can be simple signs of age, but if any appear to be speeding up, or look odd to you, be sure to contact your veterinarian.

Other Age-Related Problems

As your Great Dane moves forward in time, his body becomes more suscep-tible to illnesses, and they can take a harder toll on him. His organs can begin to develop problems. Some things that can be more problematic with age include the following:

- **Diarrhea and vomiting**—Each cause severe dehydration and can quickly take their toll on older dogs. They may also indicate another serious problem.
- **Urinary tract disease**—A variety of diseases can affect his urinary sys-tem. Inflammation, cancer, and foreign bodies of the genitals can cause everything from incontinence to an increase in hunger.
- **Acquired megaesophagus**—The throat muscles fail to push food to the stomach. Special feeding needs are required for him to eat and digest food.
- **Hypothyroidism**—A reduction in thyroid pro-duction that can cause a decrease in activity, aggression, and intolerance to cold weather. Often strikes dogs over four years old.
- **Cardiomyopathy**—This is a heart disease wherein the heart muscle becomes weakened and does not function fully. Most Great Danes will develop heart failure from this.
- **Fatty deposits or lipomas**—These benign tumors create lumps, tags, and bumps on older dogs. Veterinarians usually leave them alone if they are simply a fatty deposit. But these should be watched for change in size, shape, or color.
- **Hyperadrenocorticism (Cushing's disease)**—This has a variety of symptoms, from change in sleep patterns to decreased responsiveness to commands to reduced activity levels.
- **Cancer**—This can strike at any age, but is a common source for the loss of an elderly Great Dane. The worst is probably osteosarcoma, or bone cancer, which mostly affects the giant breeds, like Great Danes. Appear-ing as swelling in the shoulder, wrist, or knee, once discovered it has, sadly, already spread. Also deadly is hemangiosarcoma, which affects the linings of blood vessels.

Many of these can be treated with medication. However, as your dog ages, you need to begin considering the side effects of such medication. Sometimes they can make his life less comfortable. This is something he does not need as he ages.

Saying Good-bye . . .

At any age, after your Great Dane departs, it is important to decide what you want to have done with his empty shell. As he may be comparable to the size of some humans, it can be a more difficult, and costly, process that requires some planning. Veterinarians usually have plans for unclaimed bodies that can range from mass cremations to landfills and/or rendering plants. You may want to consider private burial or cremation.

Some owners may have enough land and strength to bury a 100-plus-pound Great Dane when local ordinances allow for such. Others may wish to look into a pet cemetery. Many pet cemeteries handle all the details, from retrieving the body to performing a ceremony where family and friends can pay their respects. Remember, the size of an adult Great Dane will make the costs for almost any dignified ending higher than those for smaller breeds. A cemetery plot cost would include purchase and necessary accessories such as a case (coffin) and marker (tombstone). This expense could run between $1,500 and $2,500 with an annual upkeep of $30 a year or more.

Cremation services are offered by many pet cemeteries. (Your veterinarian may be able to arrange this service for you.) A cremation service for a Great Dane can run $100 to $300 or more. Cremation allows one the option to keep the ashes at home, or possibly scatter them in areas he truly loved. There are even hollow necklace pendants and other jewelry pieces available that are designed to hold a small amount of ashes or fur so you may keep your departed friend with you at all times.

Chapter Ten

The Great Dane Standard

Great Danes are Great Danes in any language. However, it does seem that there are different beliefs of where the Great Dane truly fits in the conformation showing world.

The Great Dane is part of the Working Dog Group in the American Kennel Club, the Association Japan Kennel Club, The Kennel Club (British), and the Canadian Kennel Club. He has been placed in the Non-Sporting Group in the New Zealand Kennel Club, Australian Kennel Club, and the Kennel Club of Southern Africa. Great Danes also find themselves part of the Guardian Group within the United Kennel Club. The Fédération Cynologique Internationale classifies him in Group 2 Pinscher and Schnauzer type, Molossian type, and Swiss Mountain and Cattle Dogs.

Why Is There a "Standard"?

Standards are more than just a list of physical attributes that judges look for in a show ring. They are a combination of elements that make the Great Dane unique among other dogs. When people look at a well-bred Great Dane, they should instantly recognize it for the majestic dog that he is.

The standard is used so that all Great Danes (and any officially recognized breed) can be judged on an equal playing field. When judges step into the ring, they will not pick a dog that they think looks "good." They should pick the dog that most closely matches that standard.

"The Great Dane combines, in its regal appearance, dignity, strength and elegance with great size and a powerful, well-formed, smooth muscled body. It is one of the giant working breeds, but is unique in that its general conformation must be so well balanced that it never appears clumsy, and shall move with a long reach and powerful drive."—Excerpt from the American Kennel Club's Great Dane Standard.

The Great Dane standard is the basis for the perfect dog originally developed to hunt and protect. To succeed, a Great Dane was given the following characteristics:

- Great size and physical strength to take down quarry or prey.
- Long, muscled legs that could effortlessly allow him to traverse long distances.

149

- Short, straight back for overall balance, to maximize movements and permit swift maneuvering.
- Broad-based, long, tapered tail used in rudder-like fashion to help with tight turns.
- Strong, arched neck to back up the jaw's grip and shake even heavy game.
- Large, strong jaws with a scissors bite and full dentition, for maximum biting and holding ability.

Measuring the Great Dane

The Great Dane is a giant breed. Breed clubs around the world expect males to be at least 30 inches (76 cm) at the shoulder, and bitches at least 28 inches (71 cm). Yet some places expect him to get to this height sooner rather than later. With American Kennel Club sanctioned shows Great Dane puppies as young as six months of age are expected to reach this minimum height to be exhibited in conformation. The Australian Nation Kennel Association, the New Zealand Kennel Club, and the Kennel Club of Southern Africa's Standard list 18 months when minimum height is reached.

Height requirements don't appear to be an issue for owners showing their Great Dane puppies at International All Breed Canine Association shows

FYI: Bigger Isn't Necessarily Better

While a Great Dane's size is mostly determined by his genetics, prepubertal gonadectomy or desexing before puberty (often done before 16 weeks of age) removes important hormones, which can delay the closing of his growth plates. Growth plates are areas of developing cartilage tissue near the ends of long bones that determine the ultimate length and even shape of the bone.

Growth occurs around the growth plate and not from the center of the bone outward like one might think. When a dog is full grown, the growth plates "close" by hardening into bone. The delay in this growth plate closure is what often creates taller, leggier dogs. In large or giant breeds this can be a problem as a lot of growth can occur, increasing the risk of orthopedic disorders such as hip dysplasia, cruciate ligament disease, and even bone cancer. If a Great Dane is neutered when he's 9 months of age, his femur (the thigh bone, which runs hip to knee) may have reached its genetically determined length, but perhaps his tibia (the bone that runs knee to hock) continues to grow because it does not get the signal to stop when it should. This example creates an odd angle of the stifle (knee), which in turn can put increased stress on joints or even the ligaments. (Ligaments are flexible tissues that connect bones or cartilages together at a joint.) This stress in turn can lead to a higher rate of ligament tears or ruptures.

See Chapter 4 for more on spaying and neutering.

since puppies and adults compete at different levels and for different titles. Puppies as young as three months of age can be shown at IABCA events, so the height part of the standard just seems to be kindly overlooked for them.

The AKC Great Dane standard does also list that 2 inches or more than these minimums are preferred, providing that the dog is well proportioned to his height. Great Danes should be balanced in overall appearance, not resemble a canine giraffe. As there is no maximum height restriction in Great Danes (as there are in some breeds), their height can vary, though on average bitches are 30 to 33 inches (76–84 cm) tall, whereas male dogs are 33 to 36 inches (76–91 cm) tall.

How do you measure a Great Dane? First have your Great Dane stand on a fully flat surface. An even sidewalk or driveway is ideal, as he'll have better traction on it than on a slick surface like linoleum. Second, feel where his withers are. This is where the back of his neck meets his shoulder blades. You should be able to feel the "points" of his shoulders through his short coat. This is where you are going to measure him. Before measuring you'll want to show the yardstick to your Great Dane so he'll have less interest in it when you are measuring him. If you raise the stick over his head or move it too rapidly, he may get nervous, which could make getting a proper measurement difficult should he crouch, arch his topline, or fail to stand.

Once ready keep the Great Dane standing square with his head as level as possible. Place one end of the yardstick on the even ground just behind the Great Dane's front leg as the rest of it points skyward. Place your ruler across his withers, keeping the ruler as level as you can. Line your ruler against the yardstick and with a pencil mark the yardstick where the underside of the ruler touched it. Now, read the yardstick mark or measure the length of your makeshift measuring stick. This is how tall he is. If you plan to check your dog's height frequently, you may consider purchasing a U-shaped device created specifically for the task, called a wicket. Wickets are often used at conformation dog shows by judges who question the height of an exhibited dog.

The Head of Apollo

The Great Dane's head should be rectangular, long, distinguished, expressive, and finely chiseled—especially under the eyes. Viewed from the side the head resembles a brick resting on top of another in that the plane of the skull and plane of the muzzle are straight and parallel to one another. The forehead is sharply set off from the bridge of the nose in what is called a strongly pronounced stop. The skull plane slopes into a smooth line into a full, square, deep muzzle.

FYI: Great Dane Movement

In the conformation show ring Great Danes are moved at a trot.

During this gait a judge is watching the following:

- The dog as a whole, as he should move with confidence, carrying his tail out but never straight up or over the back.
- The front legs, as they should have long reach, with the front paw landing below the dog's nose.
- The rear legs, as they should have powerful drive, pushing off strongly. The rear paw landing as if overlapping the invisible track of the same side front paw.
- The back, as it should appear level with no tossing, rolling, or bouncing.
- From the front or the rear the legs should not twist in or outward at the elbow or hock joints.

- **The Eyes:** Almond shaped, medium in size, deep set, and dark with a lively intelligent expression. Blue or partially blue eyes are permitted in the Harlequin.
- **The Ears:** High set and medium in size, folded forward and close to the cheek. If cropped the length is in proportion to the size of the head and carried erect.
- **The Lips:** Squared off of the deep muzzle.
- **The Nose:** Shall be black except in the Blue, where it is dark blue-black. Black spotted is permitted in the Harlequin.
- **The Teeth:** Strong well developed with full dentition. The front teeth fit together in a scissors bite, resembling the blades of scissors where the top jaw teeth fit close but in front of the lower.

The Body of a Great Dane

A Great Dane should be somewhat boxlike with legs and back creating a square. It starts with a broad, deep chest that is well muscled without a pronounced sternum (breast bone). The trunk needs to be short, level, and with a broad loin. The underline of the body should be tightly muscled with a well-defined tuck-up. The shoulder blades should be strong and sloping (downward slant).

- **The Neck:** High set, long, well arched, and muscular. Gradually broadening from the nape and smoothly flowing into the withers (the highest part of the back, behind the neck and between the shoulders).
- **The Upper Arm:** Strong, muscular, and close fitting. Upper tip of the shoulder to the back of the elbow joint is perpendicular.
- **The Forearm:** Strong, muscular, and straight. Elbow is one-half the distance from the withers to the ground.
- **The Pasterns:** Strong and sloping slightly

- **The Front Feet:** Cat-like, round, compact, and well-arched toes. Toeing neither in nor out. Nails short and dark as possible.
- **The Hindquarters:** Strong, broad, muscular, and well angled with well let down hocks.
- **The Hocks:** Strong, straight, and sturdy. Seen from the rear turn neither inward nor outward.
- **The Hind Feet:** Round and compact with well-arched toes, neither toeing in or out. Nails short and dark as possible.
- **The Croup:** Broad and slightly sloping.
- **The Tail:** A continuation of the spine that is set high and smoothly into the croup. Broad at the base, tapering down to the hock joint. When excited or active may curve saber-like but not above the level of the back.

Looking at the Front

When looking your Great Dane face to face, his skull appears narrow with the bridge of his nose as broad as possible. The cheek muscles are not prominent. The chest is as deep as the elbow. Elbows are close to the body. His rib cage is well sprung. Wrists and legs are straight.

Your Great Dane won't have to measure up exactly to these points since you undoubtedly love him for who he is regardless. But it is fun to see how many of his traits are the same ones chosen centuries ago.

A Breed of Many Classes and Colors

Great Danes are one breed, if not the breed, of dog with the most conformation show class divisions in the American Kennel Club. Many breeds exhibit in a total of seven classes (in each gender) such as Puppy 6–9 Months, Puppy 9–12 Months, Puppy 12–18 Months, American Bred, Novice, Amateur-Owner-Handler, Bred by Exhibitor, and Open. The Great Dane has a total of 14 class divisions with the addition of the six individual colors.

The six conformation show colors are as follows:

- **Black**—A Black Great Dane is one with a deep, jet black colored coat. Solid black is preferred over those with white toes, a small white marking on their chest, and/or behind their paw pads.
- **Blue**—A Blue Great Dane is one with a dark steel gray, almost metallic color of coat. Solid Blue is preferred over those with white toes, a small white marking on their chest, and/or behind their paw pads.
- **Brindle**—A Brindle Great Dane typically has a yellow gold base coat with dark black striping in a chevron pattern and a black face called a mask. Distinct and even striping is preferred as is an intensive base color. Undesirable are brindles with too much or too little striping. Small white markings on toes, chest, and behind paw pads are not preferred.
- **Fawn**—A Fawn Great Dane typically has a golden base coat with a black face called a mask. A deep golden yellow is preferred over lighter shades. Smutty or black fronted Fawns are not desirable. White markings on the toes, chest, or behind the paw pads are not preferred.

- **Harlequin**—A Harlequin Great Dane has a white base coat and black torn looking patches irregularly placed upon its body. A white neck is preferred. The patches on a Harlequin should not be so large that they resemble a blanket or too small to look like dappling. Some merle (light to dark gray, often resembling an oil stain) patches are expected. NOTE: In countries such as Great Britain, Australia, New Zealand, and Africa the Blue Harlequin, white with blue patches, is also shown.
- **Mantle**—A Mantle Great Dane is strictly black and white with a black blanket over the body, having a black skull with white muzzle. A white blaze (stripe between the eyes) is optional. A whole white ring around the neck called a collar is preferred. White should extend down the chest, be on part or whole of the fore and hind legs and the tip end of the black tail. Acceptable is a small white marking in the black blanket as well as a break in the white collar.

Temperament

Although looks are certainly important, and what judges will mainly examine, temperament is even more important when thinking of adding a new family member. Though some Great Dane standards vary from country to country, all breed clubs clearly agree on what one should expect from the Apollo of Dogs:

- **American Kennel Club**—"Must be spirited, courageous, always friendly and dependable and never timid or aggressive"
- **Canadian Kennel Club**—"Spirited and courageous—never timid"
- **Fédération Cynologique Internationale**—"A self-assured, unafraid, easily guided and docile companion"
- **United Kennel Club**—"Spirited, courageous, friendly and dependable"
- **The Kennel Club**—"Kindly without nervousness, friendly and outgoing"

In the past the Great Dane needed courage and spirit to do his job well, whether that was as a hunter of wild game or as a protector and guardian of his master's estate. In today's world that courage is still appreciated, as the Great Dane may help his owners feel more at ease just with the knowledge that he is beside them. The deep resonating bark of a Great Dane alone can give would-be troublemakers reason to pause or turn tail. Yet it is the breed's friendly and dependable nature that truly wins the hearts of millions.

Resources

Great Dane Web Pages

6Star Danes—General information
www.6stardanes.com

Great Dane Club of America—
official Great Dane Club
of the United States
www.gdca.org

Leans & Slobbers—discussion board
www.leansnslobbers.proboards.com

Uncropped Great Dane
Champions—information site
*http://sharlaitdanes.com/Galleries/
Natural_Champions/Natural_
Champions.html*

Health and Research

AKC Canine Health Foundation
www.akcchf.org

Morris Animal Foundation
www.morrisanimalfoundation.org

Nutrition

Animal Food Services—supplier of
raw diets to zoos and the general
public
www.animalfood.com

Aunt Jeni's Home Made—raw and
organic food supplier
Auntjeni.com/barf.htm

Barfworld.com—raw food supplier
and information site
www.barfworld.com

www.dogfoodanalysis.com
Independent review of all dog food
ingredients and nutrition

www.dogfoodscoop.com
Compares, reviews, and rates commercial dog foods

Dr. Ian Billinghurst—Veterinarian
and raw food advocate
www.barfaustralia.com

rawlearning.com—comprehensive
information site on raw feeding
www.rawlearning.com

National Dog Clubs
and Organizations

American Kennel Club
www.akc.org

International All Breed Canine
Association
www.iabca.com

United Kennel Club
www.ukcdogs.com

Index

A

Accidents, 49–50
Adoption, 36
Affection, 16, 24, 64, 82
Age-related problems, 145–146
Aggression, 58, 64–65, 72, 111
Agility, 30, 41, 115–116
Aging dog, 16, 119. *See also* senior dog
Air travel, 50
American Kennel Club, 27, 31, 103, 116–117, 119, 149–151, 154–155
Anus, 58–59, 78, 95
Anxiety, 64, 76–77, 79, 91, 96
  barking, 72
Arthritis, 98, 140, 144

B

Barking, 21–22, 71–72, 76, 108–109, 111, 142
Bathing, 129–130
Bedding, 51, 67
Biting, 25, 45, 72–73, 74, 94
Blankets, 67, 82–83, 94, 110, 114, 140, 142
Bloat, 95–97
Boarding facilities, 113
Body, 18–19, 153–154
  language, 18–19, 111
  posture, 64
Bone cancer, 97–98
Bone diseases, 61–62
Boredom, 72, 77, 119
Breed, 1–3
Breeders, 30–35, 41

C

Canadian Kennel Club, 149, 155

Cancer, 59, 79, 85, 95, 97–98, 145
Canine Good Citizen program, 114–115
Canine Health Information Center, 38
Cardiomyopathy, 145
Car travel, 110
Cemetery plot, 147
Chewing, 45, 51, 72, 77, 98, 132
Children, 13, 21, 74, 82–83, 109, 112
Clicker, 71, 101–102
Climate, local, 82
Coat, 37, 82–83
Coat for cold weather, 83
Cognitive dysfunction syndrome, 142
Collar, 51, 68–70, 102, 109
Color, 12, 27–29, 31–32, 154–155
Colostrum, 52
Come command, 103–104
Command "cue" word, 101, 105
Commands, 15, 103–107
Companionship, 15–16, 40
Compatibility of breed, 24
Conformation, 41, 118–119
Constipation, 144
Costs, 16, 30, 36, 87, 91, 146–147
Crate, 20, 25, 50–51, 110
Cremation, 147
Crying, 45, 62, 72
Cushing's disease, 145

D

Dewclaws, 38
De-worming, 54–55
Diarrhea, 37, 95, 145
Digging, 76–77
Distemper, 53

Dog
  cot, 139
  food, 86–91, 157
  license, 113
  other, 22–23
  shows, 28, 41, 119
Down command, 106
Drooling, 20, 58, 72, 76, 96, 101, 136

E

Ear, 12, 18–19, 64, 132–133, 141–142, 153
  cropping, 52, 55–58, 157
  mites, 133
Energy levels, 24, 40, 140
Exercise, 24, 98, 113, 116–117, 140
Eyes, 18–19, 37–38, 64, 80–81, 141–142, 153

F

Facial expression, 64
Fear, 40, 44, 65, 75
Feeding
  puppy, 60–61
  senior dog, 143
First Aid kit, 114
Flees, 135–136
Food, 15, 16, 85–89
Full moon, 98

G

Genetics, 85, 151
Good-bye, saying, 146–147
Grass eating, 98
Great Dane(s)
  choosing, 28, 30
  in films, 7–9
  name origin, 12
  questions about, 12–13
  of rich and famous, 6
  standard for, 149–155
  timeline, 11

Great Dane Club of America, 3–4, 11, 31, 55, 60, 157
Great Dane Club of California, 4, 7, 31
Great Dane clubs, 31
Great Dane Gazette, 31
Great Dane Review, 31
Grooming, 24, 129–130, 144
Guinness Book of World Records, 10–11, 13
Gums, 89, 93, 96, 98

H

Hair care, 129–30
Hall of Fame, 3–7
Harlequins, 7, 12, 28

Head, 18–19, 152–153
Health
  about, 15, 30, 32, 37
  guarantees, 34
  insurance, 59, 91
  issues, 92–97
  tests, 38–39
Hearing, 79
Heart, 38, 85
Heat exhaustion, 110
Heel command, 104–105
Height, 13, 43, 74–75, 150
High five, 107–108
Hip dysplasia, canine, 38, 85, 98–99
Hip muscle loss, 141
Hotels, 113

Housetraining, 36, 47–48
Human fear, 79
Hunting, 1, 15, 79, 80–81
Hypothyroidism, 38, 58, 145

I

Internet, 30–31, 157

J

Jumping, 20, 115, 117
Junior handling class, 118

K

The Kennel Club (British), 149, 155

L

Leash, 23, 25, 48, 68–70, 102, 109
  training, 122–123
Leave it command, 107
Leg-lift urination, 58–59
Lethargic behavior, 93
Life span, 13, 20, 93, 139
Lipomass (fatty deposits), 145
Lips, 18, 130, 153
Litters, 31–34, 39–40, 43, 54

M

Measurements, 150–151
Medical costs, 36, 59
Medical records, 32, 39
Medications, 94
Megaesophagus, 99, 145
Mites, 133, 137
Mouth, 18–19, 44–45, 70–73, 132

N

Nail-trimming, 134–135
Nose, 37, 79–80, 94, 117–118, 153
Nose pinch, 45
Nutrition, 52, 60, 85–86, 89, 156–157

O

Obedience, 36, 41, 116–117, 119
Overweight dog, 90–91
Owner responsibility, 20

P

Pacing, 76, 96
Pack behavior, 24, 111
Pain, 21, 61–62, 72, 74
Panting, 58, 76, 96, 98
Parasites, 90, 95, 98, 135
Paws, 51, 106
Pedicures, 134–135
Pedigree, 32, 34
Personality, 15, 18–19, 39
Pets, other, 22–25
Pet sitter, 114
Play, 21, 139
Potty, 51

Potty training, 48–50
Praise, 102, 122–126, 139
Protein, 61, 88
Pulse, 94
Punishment, 50
Puppy
  aptitude tests, 40–41
  choosing a, 36–39
  8 months, 58
  8 weeks, 34, 43–44, 52
  1st year, 43
  growth, rate of, 16
  mind of, 39–40
  6 months, 44–45
  nutrition, 60–61
  scared, 51
  16 weeks, 44–45, 53
  size, 12
  12 weeks, 34, 44, 55, 57
Puppy kindergarten, 103
Puppy-proofing house, 46
Purebred dogs, 16

Q

Quiet time, 51

R

Rabies, 53–54, 113
Rally, 117, 119
Raw diet, 89–90
Registration, 34, 38, 120
Re-owned dogs, 16
Rescue dog, 35–36
Resources, 157
Rewards, 102, 122, 124–126, 134

S

Satin Balls, 90
Scavenging, 77
Seat belts, canine, 110
Senior dog, 139–147
Separation anxiety, 62, 72, 75–77
Service dogs, 120
Shedding, 24, 129–130
Sit command, 124–125
Size, 18, 67, 91, 93, 98
Smell, 78–79
Social animal, 19–20
Socialization, 62–63, 72–73

Space needs, 12, 24
Spay/neuter, 46, 58–60, 151
Sport competitions, 115–120
Standard breed, 149–150
Stand command, 107
Stay command, 105, 126–127
Sunscreen, 82–83

T

Tail, 18–21, 65, 74–75, 111, 154
Taste, 43, 67, 81–82, 86
Teeth, 44, 51, 131–132, 153
Temperament, 30, 32, 39, 155
Temperature, 93–94
Testicles, 44
Theft, 74–75
Therapy dogs, 5, 120
Thyroid, 37–38, 145
Ticks, 136–137
Touch, 64, 82
Toys, 15, 50–51, 62, 67, 69, 114
Tracking, 117–118
Trainable dog, 15
Training, 20, 24, 46
Transportation, 20
Travel, 50
Treats. See rewards
Tricks, 107–109

U

United Kennel Club, 116, 119, 149, 155, 157
Unleashed areas, 111–112

V

Vaccination, 36, 44, 52–54, 113
Veterinarian, 38, 44, 59, 73, 91–93, 113
Veterinarian bills, 16
Vomiting, 92, 95–96, 136, 145

W

Walks, 109–110, 113, 115
Water, 20, 82, 109–110
Weight, 12, 15, 90, 95, 98
Whining, 58, 76, 96
Worms, canine, 54–55, 136

THE TEAM BEHIND THE *TRAIN YOUR DOG* DVD

Host **Nicole Wilde** is a certified Pet Dog Trainer and internationally recognized author and lecturer. Her books include *So You Want to Be a Dog Trainer* and *Help for Your Fearful Dog* (Phantom Publishing). In addition to working with dogs, Nicole has been working with wolves and wolf hybrids for over fifteen years and is considered an expert in the field.

Host **Laura Bourhenne** is a Professional Member of the Association of Pet Dog Trainers, and holds a degree in Exotic Animal Training. She has trained many species of animals including several species of primates, birds of prey, and many more. Laura is striving to enrich the lives of pets by training and educating the people they live with.

Director **Leo Zahn** is an award winning director/cinematographer/editor of television commercials, movies, and documentaries. He has directed and edited more than a dozen instructional DVDs through the Picture Company, a subsidiary of Picture Palace, Inc., based in Los Angeles.